WHEN THE BANKS SAY NO!

Use...

Streetwise Seller Financing™

Sell Your Property up to 70% Faster!

by W. Eddie Speed

Contributing Writers:
Dan Fuller and Scott Murray

Streetwise Seller Financing is designed as a complete guide to the entire process of seller financing real estate. Starting with the homework before the sale, Eddie Speed moves through underwriting, structuring the sale, complying the applicable state and federal laws, preventing default and what to do if your property does enter default.

♦ Homework Before the Sale - learn how to properly qualify your borrower to avoid default!

♦ Structuring the Sale - are you in full compliance with all the laws regarding seller-financing? Structure the sale properly and you'll not only save legal headaches, but you can ensure your investment is worth top-dollar.

♦ Dealing with Default - Eddie discusses plenty of tips and tricks to deal with a defaulting borrower. Use this section to avert disaster and help save your valuable investment.

Streetwise Seller Financing™

Published by:
Streetwise Seller Financing

Printed in the United States of America.

11   10   9   8   7   6   5   4   3   2

TABLE OF CONTENTS

Seller financing may not seem, at first glance, to be a very glamorous topic. When was the last time you pulled out the fine china for tea and a lively discussion of the legal requirements of RESPA or the appropriate structure of a real estate security document? However, consider this: seller financing is a tool that can be used to close deals faster, sell hard-to-place properties and to finance borrowers that may not qualify for traditional bank loans. At the end of the day, this business is all about selling property and this book, *Streetwise Seller Financing*, is designed as a handy guide to creating a transaction that makes both legal and financial sense. Glamorous, indeed!

The market for seller financing has matured considerably since the days of taking back a note for anyone and everyone with a little "jingle money" in their pocket. Old timers can tell you stories of financing buyers without any sort of application – just a steady job and a handshake promise to pay each month. Today's market demands a greater sophistication as the industry has become more standardized, but don't be too discouraged; as I will show you, common sense underwriting still drives the transaction. In essence, the seller financing industry has developed to the point that a seller financed real estate transaction is now a marketable commodity, just like any other. Investors of real estate paper now have at their disposal measurable statistics on industry trends, sophisticated financing models, as well as collection and servicing software. This evolution is great news for individuals holding real estate notes or for those considering selling a property and providing financing, because it allows you to help protect your investment by building in a viable exit strategy – whether you sell the loan or collect it to maturity.

But here's the caveat. Anyone who provides financing needs to commit to memory a quote from a seasoned Texas banker who once said, "The time to worry about a loan is before you make it." Consider for a moment what is being said in this phrase. If a loan is made in haste, with little forethought, planning or investigation then only luck can be counted on for a favorable outcome, and the holder will almost always severely limit his options. **The homework always has to be done on the front end!**

Therefore, the most important thing to remember for someone thinking about seller financing is that it is always in his or her best interest to:

- Qualify and gain a comfort level with the buyer prior to the sale by obtaining as much information about the buyer as possible in order to ascertain their ability to make payments and honor all other covenants of the loan documents now and in the future;

- Structure the sale and resulting note and security document in a way that is legal, provides the most protection, flexibility and marketability and facilitates an exit strategy for the seller in the event of changing circumstances;

- Develop a system that will provide organization and detailed and accurate records relating to the loan and the borrower;

- Understand and comply with all legal obligations of a seller/lender under the note and security document, as well as applicable State and Federal statues.

This book breaks down the seller financing transaction into three parts: Homework before the sale, Structuring the sale, and Preventing default after the sale. We'll discuss common sense underwriting, servicing and collection methods along with regulatory/statutory ramifications of serving in the capacity of a lender. In addition, we'll take a close look at a variety of methods to help mitigate a potential loss should you be faced with the problem of a delinquent owner-financed note. It's my hope that this book enables you to enter into a seller financed transaction with a higher level of confidence in both your buyer and in the note itself. As always, if you have any questions about anything we cover here, please consult your attorney, accountant or other qualified professional.

NOTES

Part i
HOMEWORK BEFORE
THE SALE

Should I Owner-Finance?

It may seem elementary, but the first place we should start is to determine whether a property is a good candidate to owner-finance. Many times a property owner considers using owner-financing as a quick and easy way to sell property. In fact, sometimes they ignore the questions of qualifying the buyer and properly underwriting the sale (obtaining an adequate down payment, interest rate, etc.). You can't assume that your investment is protected simply because it is secured by your property. You may be able to get the house back in the event of a foreclosure, but what if your potential buyer destroys the property?

The reality is that seller-financing a sale can and has been used as a very valuable tool in financing "sub-standard" type real estate. What does that mean? In most real estate markets – those that have fairly aggressive lender underwriting and affordable interest rates – most properties sell with a 3rd party lender qualifying the borrower and the collateral (the property) and then extending a loan. So the issue is, how can I determine if the property I'm selling falls outside of what most traditional mortgage lenders want. Secondly when can I safely owner-finance a property to a buyer with either no credit or poor credit. In other words, what down payment overrides a traditionally non-qualifiable buyer?

First let's focus on the property. Traditional third party lenders tend to shy away from single-family homes with any of the following issues: sale price range (usually under $60,000 in value), repair or condition problems, improvement to land ratio (i.e. small house on 25 acres). In addition, other types of property such as land only, used mobile home and land, and unique commercial property are all difficult to finance through a third party. If a property of any type is quickly and easily financed by a third party, why should I owner-finance it? The answer likely is I shouldn't. However, for owners of these "non-conventional" properties, owner-financing can allow the seller to receive an acceptable down payment with fewer hassles of the buyer being financed with a 3rd party. Take, for example, these two homes in Anywhere, USA:

> Home A. This property is worth $175,000 and is a 4 year old, traditional brick, 3 bedroom/2 bath home in a suburban neighborhood of a metropolitan city.

> Home B. This property is worth $52,000 and is a wood frame house over 50 years old in a mature neighborhood inside the metropolitan area. Typical buyers in the neighborhood have "no credit" but may be able to come up with 20% down.

A buyer for Home A likely can qualify for a loan, with verifiable income and good credit. Traditional financing through a 3rd party lender is often the best exit strategy for this type of property. A buyer for Home B on the other hand, may not have adequate credit or the verifiable income needed to secure a conventional mortgage loan. The 20% down, however, is his or her redeeming factor. The seller could owner-finance the buyer with the intent of selling that note soon after closing or after the buyer has made some payments.

If Home B is conventionally financed, it will have an inordinately high amount of closing costs, as a percentage of the sales price. In addition, requiring conventional financing on Home B will greatly reduce the pool of potential buyers, adding significantly to marketing time (the period from the placement of the home on the market to the signing of a purchase agreement).

The real advantage with owner-financing Home B is a much shorter time to close. The reduced paperwork involved in owner-financing versus conventional financing can shorten the closing cycle from an average of 6-8 weeks with conventional financing down to 2-3 weeks with an owner-financed property. When you consider that a vacant property typically costs you 2% of the value of the property each month in interest, taxes, insurance and general upkeep, a shorter selling time translates to significant savings. Owner-financing also means that the lender doesn't call you up on day 52 of processing and ask for "just one more thing." Many professional real estate investors can attest to the pain of hearing those words!

The basic rule of thumb is to consider how conventional financing will fit your transaction. If the "trouble factor" is too high, then why not owner-finance? The next issue is then to ensure that you are not letting someone into your property with inadequate underwriting, since the best way to handle default is to prevent it from occurring in the first place.

The Application

Underwriting all begins with the credit application. You'll want to use a form that asks all the important questions, of course, but more importantly, you'll need to verify each and every item on the application. Many lenders use the Freddie Mac Universal Loan Application

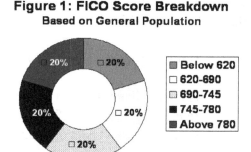

Figure 1: FICO Score Breakdown
Based on General Population

- 20% Below 620
- 20% 620-690
- 20% 690-745
- 20% 745-780
- 20% Above 780
- 20%

which is very detailed and asks all the important questions. We've placed a sample copy of the application in Appendix B. Perhaps the most important piece of information on the application is the borrower's social security number. Always ask to see the original Social Security card to verify that the number is correct. A dishonest borrower might give you an incorrect number in the hopes that you'll receive a blank report from the credit bureau.

The **employment section** of the application is of the utmost importance. More than just looking for employment gaps, you'll need to be on the lookout for out and out fraud as a dishonest borrower will frequently misrepresent his or her employment record. Verification of employment includes calling each employer for a reference, checking the length of employment, as well as the current salary. You might consider the following questions:

1.   In what type of industry does the applicant work? Is the employer a business that provides stable, year round employment, or is the business more seasonal or transitional in nature? Is the applicant's position of a short term or long-term nature?

2.   Is there much assurance that the business will be there in the long term?

3.   If the applicant is self-employed, has he been successful in earning a living sufficient to meet his monthly obligations (including the proposed financing) for more than a couple of years or is he recently self-employed?   In other words, is it likely that he will have a stable source of income for some time to come?

Once the amount of compensation is disclosed, consider how and when the applicant is paid:

1.   Is the applicant paid on a salary?

2.   Is the applicant paid on a commission only basis that may result in fluctuating income? If so, try to obtain an average monthly income for at least two years or as far back as possible.

3.   Does the applicant earn hourly wages? Know the rate per hour and obtain the average number of hours per week the borrower has worked in the past and then question the borrower as to the hours he expects to work in the future.

4.   Is the applicant paid weekly? Every two weeks? Monthly? Annually?

Please note that in many cases, the "applicant" consists of both husband and wife and their employment status will be a combination of the above mentioned scenarios; therefore the seller must take into consideration the employment and earnings of both spouses in totality to fairly and accurately determine their combined ability to pay.

Rental History - It is a prudent move to call the applicant's former landlord to verify rent payment history, as well as finding out if he caused any problems while renting his former home. You'll want to verify at least 2 years of prior payment history. Obviously, the farther you go back, the more certain you can be of their true payment history.

Reference Verification - While we're on the subject of calling references listed on the application such as former landlords, I think it's important to mention something that John Zarrella once told me which has really stuck with me. John is a well-known former property manager turned real estate investor and has dealt with literally thousands of buyer applications in his career. When he calls a former landlord or really any reference, he always asks them, "If you were in my shoes, would you loan money to ol' Joe?" He says that he's not so much interested in their answer as the way in which they answer the question. If a former employer tries to hedge the question by saying they really can't discuss questions like that, or if the chap's father-in-law tells you he wouldn't sell to the guy, you have important information to consider from people that know your borrower much better than you do.

Balance Sheet - The assets and liabilities section is the meat of the application. Verification includes checking the bank accounts and balances against what they listed on the application. You'll also want to pay special attention to the liabilities – as mentioned earlier, verification of these accounts can be found by pulling their credit report. You can either contract with a company to check the credit report or you can get the potential borrower to request their own report and give you a copy.

Credit Report – A major tool in the prevention of default and in evaluating credit risk is the credit report. I've enclosed a copy of a sample credit report (see figure 2), along with a description of the various codes you might find. When you obtain a credit report, the first thing you'll want to check is that the name and social security number match that on the loan application. The report will also list any recent employment information submitted by the credit companies. Note that employment information is only submitted to the agencies when someone applies for credit, so you might find gaps on the report. If you see overlapping employment records, that may indicate that the borrower has submitted incorrect credit applications in the past.

Figure 1 Sample Credit Report

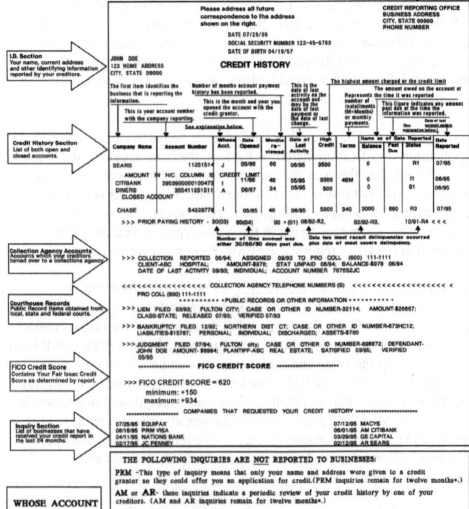

Understanding the Credit Score – A credit report will typically contain a FICO credit report score. The lowest scores are in the low 400's and the highest scores close to 850 (very few). Generally, scores exceeding 630 to 640 are considered by banks as worthy of loans. Scores below 575 are considered a high risk, and usually warrant further documentation, higher interest rates, and/or larger down payments. It has been our experience that the average credit score for buyers of owner-financed property has been fairly consistent throughout the years at around 600. In other words, the typical owner-financed sale would be considered a sub-prime sale and should involve a very careful look at the borrower's situation.

Here is a comprehensive list of the information considered by scoring models in calculating a FICO score at one of the major credit reporting agencies:

Past payment history
- Account payment information on specific types of accounts (credit cards, retail accounts, installment loans, finance company accounts, mortgage, etc.)
- Presence of adverse public records (bankruptcy, judgements, suits, liens, wage attachments, etc.), collection items, and/or delinquency (past due items)
- Severity of delinquency (how long past due)
- Amount past due on delinquent accounts or collection items
- Time since (recency of) past due items (delinquency), adverse public records (if any), or collection items (if any)
- Number of past due items on file
- Number of accounts paid as agreed

Amount of credit owing
- Amount owing on accounts
- Amount owing on specific types of accounts
- Lack of a specific type of balance, in some cases
- Number of accounts with balances
- Proportion of credit lines used (proportion of balances to total credit limits on certain types of revolving accounts)
- Proportion of installment loan amounts still owing (proportion of balance to original loan amount on certain types of installment loans)

Length of time credit established
- Time since accounts opened
- Time since accounts opened, by specific type of account
- Time since account activity

Search for and acquisition of new credit
- Number of recently opened accounts, and proportion of accounts that are recently opened, by type of account
- Number of recent credit inquiries

- Time since recent account opening(s), by type of account
- Time since credit inquiry(s)
- Re-establishment of positive credit history following past payment problems

Types of credit established

- Number of (presence, prevalence, and recent information on) various types of accounts (credit cards, retail accounts, installment loans, mortgage, consumer finance accounts, etc.)

Following the FICO score will usually be a score factor section with several numbers representing the criteria in determining the FICO score.

A 01 Current balances on accounts
B 02 Delinquency reported on accounts
C 03 Too few bank revolving accounts
D 04 Too many bank revolving accounts
E 05 Number of accounts with balances
F 06 Number of finance company accounts
G 07 Unable to evaluate recent payment history
H 08 Number of recent inquiries
I 33 Proportion of current loan balance to original loan amount
J 09 Number of accounts opened in the last twelve months
K 10 Proportion of balance to high credit on banking revolving or all revolving accounts
L 11 Current balances on revolving accounts
M 12 Length of revolving account history
N 13 Length of time (or unknown time) since account delinquent
O 14 Length of time accounts have been established
P 15 Insufficient or lack of banking revolving account information
Q 16 Insufficient or lack of revolving account information
R 17 No recent (non-mortgage) account balance information
S 18 Number of accounts delinquent
T 19 Too few rated accounts current
U 24 Lack of recently reported balances on revolving/open accounts
V 20 Length of time since legal item filed or collection item reported
W 21 Amount past due to accounts
Y 32 No recent installment loan information
Z 30 Length of time since most recent account established

* 37   Number of finance company accounts established relative to length of finance history
* 25   Length of installment loan history
* 26   Number of revolving accounts
* 99   Lack of recent history on finance accounts, or lack of finance accounts
* 31   Too few accounts with recent payment history
* 28   Number of accounts established
* 98   Lack of recent information on auto loan, or lack of auto loans
* 36   Length of time open installment loans have been established
X 38   Serious delinquency and public record or collection filed
X 39   Serious delinquency
X 40   Derogatory public record or collection filed

Public Record Information – In this section of the credit report, you'll find a record of any financial activity presented in court, such as bankruptcy, judgments, civil lawsuits and/or liens. This information will include: the reporting account's name and number; original filing date with court; status date if satisfied, released, vacated, discharged or dismissed; amount and type of public record; certificate or docket number; and code describing the borrower's relation to the public record item.

Trades Information – The trades section of the credit report features detailed information about all the installment accounts and liabilities that the borrower has undertaken, along with full payment history. Each listing includes the name of the account, date opened, last reported activity, high credit amount (either the loan amount, or credit limit), monthly payment and balance information, and any delinquencies reported. The most common of the codes used to describe an accounts condition are as follows:

CURR ACCT	ACCOUNT IS CURRENT IN PAYMENTS AND IN GOOD STANDING
CUR WAS 30-3	ACCOUNT IS CURRENT WAS THIRTY DAYS LATE THREE TIMES
PAID	ACCOUNT HAS BEEN PAID OFF TO A ZERO BALANCE AND IS INACTIVE

CHARGOFF	UNPAID BALANCE HAS BEEN REPORTED AS LOSS BY CREDIT GRANTOR AND ARE NO LONGER SEEKING REIMBURSEMENT
COLLECT	ACOUNT IS SERIOUSLY PAST DUE AND ASSIGNED TO COLLECTIONS
FORECLOS	PROPERTY WAS FORECLOSED
BKLIQREQ	DEBT FORGIVEN THROUGH CHAPTER 7, 11, OR 13
DELINQ 90	ACCOUNT IS NINETY DAYS PAST DUE
INACTIVE	ACCOUNT IS INACTIVE
CLOSED	ACCOUNT IS CLOSED

Sources of Public Records – If you need to gather information about your borrower either in the application stage or in the collection stage, you'll want to make use of public records. By using these records, you can determine where a person is living, what he or she owns, criminal records, etc. You may want to begin your search with a quick scan of the online databases that many states and counties have made available for access over the Internet (www.brbpub.com/pubrecsites.asp). If you're looking for real estate records, just visit the county recorder's office at the courthouse (or wherever records are housed in your state). You can check on liens, property records, information on land bought or sold, as well as other public information such as judgments against the borrower, marriage and divorce documents, and DBA certificates. If you're researching someone who lived in a distant county, you might want to consider hiring a local document retriever who will search the records for you for a fee.

Common Sense Underwriting

Underwriting Food for Thought is a set of very general questions that you can use when constructing an owner-financed package. Banks and other large lenders have developed guidelines through extensive research to help them determine what constitutes an acceptable level of risk. If you later decide to cash out your mortgage and sell the payments to a note buyer, they also use these questions to determine the amount that they're able to give you for your future payments. The ideal borrower will be able to answer "no" to all of these questions; however, a few "yes" answers doesn't necessarily mean you have to scrap the deal. What each "yes" answer does mean is a higher level of risk. Using these questions as a guide will help you determine how you should structure your note.

- **Is the borrower's credit score less than 580?**
  The credit score is, of course, one of the most important determining factors in evaluating a borrower. A low credit score is a serious derogatory mark and would require considerable redeeming factors (large down payment, extenuating life circumstances, etc). Keep in mind that from a note investor's standpoint, if the answer to this question is yes, the likelihood of selling this note unseasoned is very low.
- **Are all the borrower's credit report trade lines less than 6 months old?**
  This question involves looking at the trades section of the credit report to determine the length of their credit accounts. An ideal borrower would have a good pay history over a considerable amount of time. A credit report full of only new and/or closed accounts would need to be evaluated carefully.
- **Has the borrower had a bankruptcy in the past 3 years or more than 2 in their lifetime?**
- **Has the borrower had a foreclosure in the past 5 years?**
  This is common sense underwriting at it's best. However, you'd be surprised at the number of sellers that don't take past foreclosures into account. You might think that a foreclosure doesn't really matter since you get the property back and can resell it. But what if your borrower leaves your property in terrible condition?
- **Does the borrower have an existing mortgage that's not reflected on the credit report?**
  Verification of the borrower's application becomes important here. If they indicate that they rented their previous home, I'd want to see verification to that effect.
- **Has the borrower been with the same employer for less than 1 year OR in the same line of business for less than 3 years?**
  As the old saying goes, employment stability can cure many ills. A general understanding of your community's job market doesn't hurt either. If your borrower has a specialized job working in a one factory town, you'd want to be reasonably sure that the company will be around next year.
- **Will the property be non-owner occupied?**

If your borrower intends to turn your home into a rental property, you have to understand that your investment is at a higher risk. A larger down payment with a higher minimum credit score would be in order. If the borrower isn't living in the house, there is less incentive to maintain the property. Also, if your borrower runs into financial difficulty, they will be more likely to default on property where they don't personally live.

- **Is the household income less than $1500 a month?**
- **Is the debt to income ratio greater than 50%?**
  This is defined as all the combined bills (including estimated monthly payment of subject home, 1/12th of the estimated yearly property taxes and insurance, and the second lien payment if applicable) shown as a percentage of the overall gross verified income, before taxes. A debt to income ratio much higher than 50% will make it nearly impossible for your borrower to pay all their obligations.

Calculating Ability to Pay – As previously mentioned, it is important to obtain an authorization from the applicant to verify employment and reported income with the employer. Once the total gross monthly income is confirmed, a lender can run some quick and easy calculations to determine the applicant's ability to repay the proposed financing. Below is one way to verify repayment ability:

The standard calculation used by many institutional mortgage lenders is called the **debt to income ratio** (sometimes called the front-end/back-end ratio). To calculate the front-end ratio, take the amount of the proposed monthly payment plus 1/12 of the annual taxes and insurance divided by the applicant's total gross monthly income. To determine the back-end ratio, take all of the fixed monthly obligations less any rent or mortgage payments that will disappear when the new loan is created, plus the proposed monthly payment, plus 1/12 of the annual taxes and insurance divided by the applicants total gross monthly income.

This calculation allows the lender to ascertain first if the applicant can make the proposed monthly payment in addition to all of his other obligations with his available income, and second, with how much margin or "cushion" can he make the payment. Acceptable front-end ratio's for institutional lenders range anywhere from 27%-30%, with back-end ratios ranging from 35%-41%, and up to 50% for some investors of owner-financed paper. However, it should be noted that the ratio analysis is only a tool in determining repayment ability and should be viewed as a part of the overall underwriting process. All other factors should be taken into account when making a loan decision.

The information needed can be obtained by referring to the application, and comparing/confirming with the information in the credit bureau report to summarize the total monthly debts/expenditures of the borrower.

For example:
The proposed sale and owner-financing are broken down as follows:

Sales price: $65,000
Down payment: 6,500
Amount of note: $58,500 @ 10% for 20 years = $564.54/month plus
1/12 annual taxes and insurance @ $120.83 = **$685.37**

The total monthly obligations per application (and verified in the credit report):
Car note: $ 375.00
Credit Cards: 250.00
School loans: 150.00
Total: $ 775.00
Plus new monthly
Note payment: **685.37**   *includes 1/12 annual tax and ins.
New total: **$1,460.37**

Total Gross Monthly Income of applicant (from application and verification with employer)

Jim's salary: $1,800.00
Sally's salary: 2,200.00
Total: **$4,000.00/month**

Therefore in this example the front-end ratio is: **$685.37/$4,000 = 17.1%** and the back-end ratio is: **$1,460.37/$4,000.00 = 36.5%**

The 5 C's of Credit can be used as an outline of your due diligence process. The 5 C's summarize proper underwriting of any loan and are broken down as follows:

1. CHARACTER: To me, character is the most important component of underwriting. Remember that no matter how good the credit report or how strong the income and assets of the applicant, if he or she is dishonest, deceptive or disregards obligations, you do not want to do business with them. Conversely, a person with strong character and a sense of responsibility can overcome many adverse circumstances that might otherwise cause problems down the road. You'll want to make every effort to get a feel for the character of the person applying for owner-financing.

2. CREDIT: How has the applicant handled his financial obligations in the past? Unless there are mitigating circumstances, the past is a good predictor of the how the applicant will perform in the future.

3. CAPITAL: Does the applicant have any savings or net worth to get through a rainy day? Does he or she have the funds necessary to make a down payment?

4. CAPACITY: Does the applicant have the ability to repay the loan from normally recurring sources of cash, i.e., sufficient income from stable employment?

5. COLLATERAL: In the realm of owner financing, the property being sold typically is the collateral. For someone providing owner-financing, it is important to know the value of the property in relation to how much is being financed. This "Loan to Value" figure should be adjusted based on the type of collateral, as we'll discuss later. This is especially true if the seller is interested in structuring a marketable note.

The 5 C's of Credit are the touchstones for which a loan decision is made. The methods and techniques to reveal the 5 C's may vary depending on different circumstances; however the methods we discussed in this section are time proven, thorough and effective ways to fully address each of the 5 C's.

NOTES

Part ii

STRUCTURING THE SALE

One of the biggest challenges facing the potential owner financed note holder is structuring the sale in a manner that will fully comply with all the various state and federal laws related to lending (TILA, RESPA, etc.). As we'll discuss, these laws apply differently depending on the number of properties you sell with owner-financing and the amount of business you generate in a year. It's also important to create a note that follows standard underwriting practices whenever possible to later allow for maximum flexibility and liquidity, as a way of limiting your financial risk. Let's take a look at some important questions sellers typically look at when structuring a sale. If the sale of the property is structured correctly, you'll allow yourself maximum flexibility in the future.

The Credit Score and Loan to Value – I mentioned earlier that the credit score is an important factor in evaluating your potential borrower. The credit score is also important in determining the actual structure of your note by governing the terms at which you can offer your note. Generally speaking, lower credit scores mean higher interest rates and a lower Loan to Value. Loan to Value (LTV) is basically defined as the amount that you are loaning the buyer expressed as a percentage of the total value (sales price) of the property. If a buyer places 5% down on your property, you are providing a mortgage at an 95% LTV. If your borrower can put down 20%, an 80% LTV is always best. However, depending on their credit score and other redeeming factors, you may choose to adjust the LTV to a figure higher than 80%. Here's a good rule of thumb for determining an appropriate risk level:

Credit Score	Maximum Recommend LTV*
580+	**80% LTV**
600+	**85% LTV**
625+	**90% LTV**

 * as discussed below, you may also carry a piggyback second lien to assist the borrower in reaching the minimum down payment

The Property Type and Loan to Value – In addition to credit scores, LTV should also be modified by the property or collateral type. Institutional lenders continually evaluate the default rates on various property types to ensure that they don't end up loaning too much money on a higher risk property. Single family "stick built" homes are the easiest to sell on the open market (which is important if the lender receives the property back in foreclosure). By contrast, singlewide mobile homes on land in a foreclosure situation are difficult to receive an acceptable recovery amount. Observations like these have led to different recommended LTV rates depending on the property type. Unfortunately, I can't give you a hard and fast rule on correlating property type and credit score. Generally, the lower the credit score, the lower the LTV; however on some properties, such as older mobile homes, a 70% LTV is pretty much standard regardless of credit score. On commercial properties, to take another example, it's difficult to work out financing altogether if the credit score is less than 625. The chart below is based on a standard 625+ credit score:

Property Type	Maximum Recommended LTV*
Single Family Stick Built	**90% LTV**
Doublewide < 10 yrs old (on land)	**80% LTV**
Other Mobile Home	**70% LTV**
Commercial	**75% LTV**

* again, in some situations, you may also carry a piggyback second lien to assist the borrower in reaching the minimum down payment.

A Word About Interest Rates – The average credit score of an owner-financed borrower is 600. Because this credit score is lower than the conventional borrower, interest rates for owner financed property are higher than FHA and conventional rates. However, the borrower typically enjoys much lower closing costs, as well as no points or bank fees that drive up the true cost of conventionally financing a property. The interest rate you charge on your property should be in keeping with the increased risk you bear.

It's important to realize that these are just standard structuring practices. If you're in a situation where your buyer is unable to meet these general requirements, please understand that your investment may be at a greater risk. Perhaps the most common reason to move outside of these guidelines is due to the buyer inability to put 20% down. If the buyer's credit ratings and pay history warrant, a smaller down payment may be acceptable, usually accompanied by a higher interest rate to help offset the risk. As the old saying goes, "How much down does Jesse James need to buy a house?" Constructing sub-prime loans can be tricky, so you may want to seek the advice of a qualified professional on your particular loan situation. Your note professional will be more than happy to help you construct a marketable note.

What is the "Right" Structure for my Note? As we mentioned, one of the most important factors in constructing a real estate note involves the Loan-to-Value (LTV). Banks and institutional investors are looking to provide loans on single family dwellings at no higher than an 80% risk (LTV). If a borrower cannot place the required 20% down, the lender typically requires Private Mortgage Insurance (PMI) to protect against default until the borrower has built up enough equity to cover the 80% figure required. If you elect to carry back a mortgage for a buyer that cannot pay 20% down, you are in effect becoming both the lender and the insurance company, placing your investment in a potentially vulnerable position.

So what can you do if you want to sell your property to someone with less than the recommended amount down? Assuming you've done your homework and the borrower is a good credit risk, I would recommend constructing two notes. The first lien is constructed at the standard LTV for their credit score while the second (also known as a **piggyback second**) covers the difference between the borrower's down payment and your LTV. For example, if your buyer has a 580 credit score and has placed 10% down, you would construct the first lien at an 80% and the second at 10%. Together the liens form a Combined Loan to Value (CLTV) of 90%. Notice that the two liens, plus the down payment, add up to 100% of the purchase price. With this arrangement, you now have an institutional-grade note with an 80% LTV, a smaller 2nd lien representing the amount that would typically be covered by PMI, and the buyer's cash down payment. Typically, your piggyback second will have either a shorter amortization period or a balloon feature, usually maturing in 5-7 years. This arrangement gives your investment a much more solid footing, and allows you much greater flexibility if you need to liquidate for whatever reason. A couple of examples should illustrate the viability of this two lien system.

Why Loan to Value is Important – Let's assume that Jane wants to seller-finance her $100,000 home. She has found a buyer, Dick, who is interested in purchasing the home but who only has $5,000 cash to place down on the property. Jane investigates Dick's credit application using the tools and techniques we described earlier and decides that he represents a reasonable credit risk with a 602 credit score and a solid employment history. Jane has two options in structuring her note:

> **Option A:** Construct one mortgage on the entire balance due ($95,000), for a LTV of 95%. At 10% interest on a 30 year term, Dick would have a monthly payment of $833.64.

> **Option B:** Using our 2 lien system above, construct one lien at 85% LTV ($85,000) and one on the difference between the first and Dick's down payment ($10,000), for a CLTV of 95%. At 10% interest on a 30 year term, Dick would have two monthly payments: payment on the first would be $745.94 and payment on the second (10% interest on a 7 year term) would be $166.01, for a total of $911.95.

As you can see, with either option, Dick is paying basically the same amount of money each month. The real benefit to this plan comes when Jane decides a year later that she would like to liquidate her note to startup a new business: Spot's Dry Cleaning (you saw it coming, right?). She approaches an investor (commonly referred to as a note buyer) and receives a quote on her note.

> **Option A:** Because the loan was structured with a 95% LTV, the loan will need to be heavily discounted to meet the investor's underwriting criteria. Jane would receive $79,000, or 83.9% of the face amount of the note.

> **Option B:** Jane has two liens on this property, so she offers her first lien to the note buyer. Because the LTV is at 85% and meets the investor's underwriting requirements, the note buyer is able to offer her a much more competitive price for her loan. Selling this note would also yield $79,000, or 92.9% of the face amount. In addition, Jane will still receive payments on her piggyback second lien.

Keep in mind that this is only an example chosen to illustrate the difference that your loan's LTV can have on the value of your note. LTV is just one of many variables that can affect the value of a note. For example, we wouldn't usually recommend constructing a piggyback lien on an unimproved land note because the lower price points typically don't help the value of the note. Of course, underwriting for owner-financing is something that is in constant flux with ever-changing market conditions. The principles, however, are very constant. If you are going to owner-finance your property, you need to have a viable exit strategy in mind. In my career, I have purchased notes from institutions and individuals for a variety of unforseen reasons. These folks thought they would never sell their note, but for reasons including tax issues, partnership reorganization, estate liquidation, accounting problems or simply for better business opportunities, all led them to the decision to sell their note. Building in your exit strategy on the front end makes good fiscal sense in any type of investment and carrying back a note on your home should be no different.

Legal Requirements for Notes

There are a variety of legal requirements to take into consideration when you structure your note. In addition to federal statues, each state has its own set of applicable finance laws that need to be considered. What follows below is a general discussion of some of the most important legal requirements. As always, please consult with a legal professional if you have any questions about your specific situation.

Real Estate Settlement Practices Act (RESPA) – This law was enacted by Congress in 1974 to address a growing concern over proper disclosure of settlement costs to a home buyer. Enforcement of the law is the responsibility of the Department of Housing and Urban Development (HUD).

Does it apply to me? – According to HUD, RESPA **does not** apply to an all cash sale, a sale where the individual home seller takes back the mortgage, a rental property transaction or other business purpose transaction. If you are making or investing more than one million dollars a year in real estate, RESPA applies to you.

Applicable Disclosures – When a borrower applies for a loan, RESPA requires the lender to send the following disclosures:

Special Information Booklet - This booklet was created by HUD to inform borrowers better understand real estate financing and the various settlement costs that are associated with a mortgage. The Booklet is available online:http://www.hud.gov/offices/hsg/ramh/res/Settlement-Booklet-January-6-REVISED.pdf.

1. Good Faith Estimate - this form is a general estimate of the various settlement costs that your borrow can expect to pay. A sample form is located in Appendix B.

2. Mortgage Servicing Disclosure Statement - this statement tells the borrower whether you intend to service the note yourself or transfer the loan to another lender.

3. HUD-1 Settlement Statement - this form is given to borrower at closing (or 1 day before closing if the borrower requests) and lists all settlement costs associated with the loan. A sample is in Appendix B.

4. Escrow account disclosures - RESPA requires lenders to submit an annual escrow statement to the borrower. We'll cover this in more detail in our Escrow section below.

Even if RESPA doesn't apply to you, we recommend using at least the HUD-1 form in conjunction with your note. The information in the form is not only helpful to the borrower, but it also provides an excellent checklist for you to ensure that all the settlement and escrow costs are covered.

Other RESPA Issues – In addition to the Settlement disclosures, RESPA prohibits anyone from giving or accepting a kickback or unearned fee in connection with an understanding that business will be referred to any person. RESPA also prohibits anyone from giving or accepting any portion, split, or percentage of any charge made or received for rendering a settlement service other than for services actually performed. The important thing to note here is that RESPA does allow you to bill for goods or services actually performed. If you have any questions about whether a charge is allowable under RESPA, you may want to view the applicable statute at http://portal.hud.gov/hudportal/documents/huddoc?id =respa_final_rule.pdf

Truth in Lending Act (TILA) – Regulation Z of the Federal Reserve is designed to inform consumers about the use of credit by requiring disclosure of the credit terms and costs. TILA also governs advertising of credit terms.

Does it apply to me? – The Act defines a Creditor, and thus someone who must comply with TILA, as someone who regularly extends consumer credit. For the purposes of TILA, "regularly" means someone extending consumer credit more than 25 times a year or more than 5 times a year for transactions secured by a dwelling. If you sell and owner finance property more than 5 times a year, TILA applies to you.

Applicable Disclosures – TILA requires the lender to provide a disclosure both at the time of application and at the time of closing. The disclosure must have the following items present:

- ☐ Name and address of creditor
- ☐ Amount financed
- ☐ Itemization of amount financed (optional, if Good Faith Estimate is provided)
- ☐ Finance charge
- ☐ Annual percentage rate (APR)
- ☐ Variable rate information
- ☐ Payment schedule
- ☐ Total of payments
- ☐ Demand feature
- ☐ Total sales price
- ☐ Prepayment policy
- ☐ Late payment policy
- ☐ Security interest
- ☐ Insurance requirements
- ☐ Certain security interest charges
- ☐ Contract reference
- ☐ Assumption policy
- ☐ Required deposit information

Typically, lenders use a standard disclosure form for TILA that covers all of the above requirements. We've included a sample form in Appendix B.

Other TILA Issues – TILA also applies to advertising of credit terms. If you are advertising directly to the consumer, the ads must disclose the APR and terms in an approved manner. You may only advertise terms that are actually available. If you state an interest rate, you must give the "annual percentage rate" using that specific term (not "APR", "%", etc). If the annual rate can be increased at a later date, your ad must state that. Generally speaking, if you advertise of the following:

a. The percentage or the amount of down payment

b. The amount of any installment payment

c. The dollar amount of the finance charge, or

d. The number of installments or the period of repayment

then you must include ALL of the following:

e. The amount or percentage of down payment;

f. The number, amount and periods of payments: AND

g. The amount of the finance charge expressed as an annual percentage rate.

Equal Opportunity Credit Act – This law is designed to ensure that all consumers are given an equal chance to obtain credit. It defines what are and are not appropriate measures of credit-worthiness.

Does it apply to me? – The EOCA applies to anyone who issues credit. If you take back a mortgage on a property, the EOCA applies to you.

Applicable Guidelines – This law is enforced by the FTC, who has supplied these guidelines on the EOCA:

When You Apply For Credit, A Creditor May Not...

☐ Discourage you from applying because of your sex, marital status, age, race, national origin, or because you receive public assistance income.

☐ Ask you to reveal your sex, race, national origin, or religion. A creditor may ask you to voluntarily disclose this information (except for religion) if you're applying for a real estate loan. This information helps federal agencies enforce anti-discrimination laws. You may be asked about your residence or immigration status.

☐ Ask if you're widowed or divorced. When permitted to ask marital status, a creditor may only use the terms: married, unmarried, or separated.

☐ Ask about your marital status if you're applying for a separate, unsecured account. A creditor may ask you to provide this information if you live in "community property" states: Arizona, California, Idaho, Louisiana, Nevada, New Mexico, Texas, and Washington. A creditor in any state may ask for this information if you apply for a joint account or one secured by property.

☐   Request information about your spouse, except when your spouse is applying with you; your spouse will be allowed to use the account; you are relying on your spouse's income or on alimony or child support income from a former spouse; or if you reside in a community property state.

☐   Inquire about your plans for having or raising children.

☐   Ask if you receive alimony, child support, or separate maintenance payments, unless you're first told that you don't have to provide this information if you won't rely on these payments to get credit. A creditor may ask if you have to pay alimony, child support, or separate maintenance payments.

When Deciding To Give You Credit, A Creditor May Not...

☐   Consider your sex, marital status, race, national origin, or religion.

☐   Consider whether you have a telephone listing in your name. A creditor may consider whether you have a phone.

☐   Consider the race of people in the neighborhood where you want to buy, refinance or improve a house with borrowed money.

☐   Consider your age, unless:

    ☐   you're too young to sign contracts, generally younger than 18 years of age;

    ☐   you're 62 or older, and the creditor will favor you because of your age;

    ☐   it's used to determine the meaning of other factors important to creditworthiness. For example, a creditor could use your age to determine if your income might drop because you're about to retire;

    ☐   it's used in a valid scoring system that favors applicants age 62 and older. A credit-scoring system assigns points to answers you provide to credit application questions. For example, your length of employment might be scored differently depending on your age.

When Evaluating Your Income, A Creditor May Not...

☐   Refuse to consider public assistance income the same way as other income.

☐   Discount income because of your sex or marital status. For example, a creditor cannot count a man's salary at 100 percent and a woman's at 75 percent. A creditor may not assume a woman of childbearing age will stop working to raise children.

☐   Discount or refuse to consider income because it comes from part-time employment or pension, annuity, or retirement benefits programs.

☐   Refuse to consider regular alimony, child support, or separate maintenance payments. A creditor may ask you to prove you have received this income consistently.

You Also Have The Right To...

☐   Have credit in your birth name (Mary Smith), your first and your spouse's last name (Mary Jones), or your first name and a combined last name (Mary Smith-Jones).

☐   Get credit without a cosigner, if you meet the creditor's standards.

☐   Have a cosigner other than your husband or wife, if one is necessary.

☐   Keep your own accounts after you change your name, marital status, reach a certain age, or retire, unless the creditor has evidence that you're not willing or able to pay.

☐   Know whether your application was accepted or rejected within 30 days of filing a complete application.

☐   Know why your application was rejected. The creditor must give you a notice that tells you either the specific reasons for your rejection or your right to learn the reasons if you ask within 60 days.

☐   Acceptable reasons include: "Your income was low," or "You haven't been employed long enough." Unacceptable reasons are: "You didn't meet our minimum standards," or "You didn't receive enough points on our credit-scoring system." Indefinite and vague reasons are illegal, so ask the creditor to be specific.

☐   Find out why you were offered less favorable terms than you applied for—unless you accept the terms. Ask for details. Examples of less favorable terms include higher finance charges or less money than you requested.

☐   Find out why your account was closed or why the terms of the account were made less favorable unless the account was inactive or delinquent.

Source: Federal Trade Commission

Home Mortgage Disclosure Act – The HMDA was enacted by Congress in 1975 and is implemented by the Federal Reserve's Regulation C. Primarily for large, institutional lenders, this Act allows the Federal Reserve to determine if lending institutions are meeting the needs of their communities and to identify possible discriminatory lending patterns.

Does this apply to me? – The HMDA applies only to those initiating over 100 mortgages a year, or with over $10 million in assets. If this is the case, you may learn more about HMDA reporting obligations at http://www.ffiec.gov/hmda/default.htm.

Gramm-Leach-Bliley Act – This Act deals with financial institution disclosure of nonpublic personal information. It is enforced by the Federal Trade Commission.

Does this apply to me? – "Financial Institution" for the purposes of the GLBA is defined pretty broadly and includes essentially any businesses engaged in the sale of any type of financial services or products, including, banking, lending, securities or insurance products or services. If you are engaged in seller financing by trade (as opposed to someone holding back a mortgage on their former residence), you may be considered a Financial Institution. The full definition can be found in section 12 of the US Code, paragraph 1843(k). http://www4.law.cornell.edu/uscode/12/1843.html

Applicable Guidelines – The Gramm-Leach-Bliley Act (aka Privacy Act) stipulates that nonpublic personal information cannot be disclosed to a non-affiliated 3rd party unless:

A) the financial institution clearly and conspicuously discloses to the consumer, in writing or in electronic form, that such information may be disclosed to such third party;

(B) the consumer is given the opportunity, before the time that such information is initially disclosed, to direct that such information not be disclosed to such third party; and

(C) the consumer is given an explanation of how the consumer can exercise that non-disclosure option.

Regardless of whether or not a firm plans to sell the data, annual disclosure of the institution's privacy policy is required (in addition to the disclosure at the time of the initial transaction).

Fair Credit Reporting Act – This Act deals with the use of Credit Reports and is enforced by the Federal Trade Commission.

Does this apply to me? – If you are using investigative consumer credit reports in the process of approving your borrower for a mortgage, then the FCRA applies to you.

Applicable Guidelines – When the credit report is pulled, the FCRA states that disclosure must be made to the consumer that an investigative consumer report may be made. The disclosure must be in writing and mailed or otherwise delivered not later than three days after the date of the credit report request. The disclosure must include a statement "informing the consumer of his right to request the additional disclosures provided for under subsection (b) of this section and the written summary of the rights of the consumer prepared pursuant to section 609(c)." This additional disclosure is "a complete and accurate disclosure of the nature and scope of the investigation requested" and should be mailed not later than 5 days after the consumer request. The FTC has prepared a "Notice to Users of Credit Reports," which we have provided in Appendix B.

State Laws – Complicating matters are the various state laws affecting real estate transactions. By way of illustration, we've chosen a few states for further discussion, however you will certainly want to consult your applicable state statutes for information relevant to your jurisdiction.

Texas –
- Seller may not construct a contract that contains a pre-payment penalty.
- Seller may not charge a late fee that exceeds the lesser of 8% of the

monthly payment or the actual administrative costs of processing the late payment.

- Seller may not prohibit the purchaser from pledging the property as security on a future loan, such as a home equity loan.
- Annexation Disclosure. Anyone selling property outside of a municipality's corporate limits, must provide the following disclosure:

NOTICE REGARDING POSSIBLE ANNEXATION

If the property that is the subject of this contract is located outside the limits of a municipality, the property may now or later be included in the extraterritorial jurisdiction of a municipality and may now or later be subject to annexation by the municipality. Each municipality maintains a map that depicts its boundaries and extraterritorial jurisdiction. To determine if the property is located within a municipality's extraterritorial jurisdiction or is likely to be located within a municipality's extraterritorial jurisdiction, contact all municipalities located in the general proximity of the property for further information.

- Seller Disclosure of Property Condition. We've placed a sample form from the Texas Real Estate Commission in Appendix B. This form must be filled out and delivered to the buyer at the time the contract is executed.
- High interest rate loans. If the interest rate on your note is greater than 12%, Chapter 343 of the Texas Finance Code requires the following disclosures: (1) a statement regarding the value of mortgage counseling before taking out a home loan; (2) a list of the nearest available housing counseling agencies approved by the United States Department of Housing and Urban Development; (3) a list of other resources where mortgage information can be found, including toll-free telephone numbers and online resources; and (4) other disclosures required by the finance commission, including an official notice regarding high-cost home loans.
- Annual Accounting Statement. Note that if you structure your sale using a Contract for Deed, Texas law requires that the seller of property send the borrower an annual statement which must be postmarked by January 31st of each year. The statement must contain (1) the amount paid under the contract; (2) the remaining amount owed under the contract; (3) the number of payments remaining under the contract; (4) the amounts paid to taxing authorities on the purchaser's behalf if collected by the seller; (5)

the amounts paid to insure the property on the purchaser's behalf if collected by the seller; (6) if the property has been damaged and the seller has received insurance proceeds, an accounting of the proceeds applied to the property; and (7) if the seller has changed insurance coverage, a legible copy of the current policy. *For this reason, we do not recommend sellers in Texas use the Contract for Deed structure.*

California –

- Late fee cannot exceed 6% of the monthly payment, or $5, whichever is greater. Fee may not be assessed unless payment is more than 10 days overdue.
- Before the first late fee can be assessed, California law requires the lender to send a notice of delinquency to the borrower. The borrower has 10 days from the date of the letter to cure the delinquency without penalty.
- Annual accounting statement must be sent to the borrower within 60 days after the first of the year detailing the payments made into and out of a trust or escrow account.
- Seller may not construct a contract that contains a pre-payment penalty.
- Escrow accounts must be held at a California bank (exceptions exist for qualified institutions such as banks, government agencies, licensed mortgage brokers, etc.)
- Real Estate Transfer Disclosure Statement (TDS). This form details the condition of the property to the buyer. A sample may be viewed at http://www.car.org/media/pdf/legal/standard-forms/478218/
- Natural Hazard Disclosure Form. This form is designed to inform the borrower of any unusual natural conditions that may be likely to occur (Flood plain, high fire risk, earthquake risk zone, etc).
- Window Bar disclosures. A seller must disclose on the TDS the existence of any window bars and any safety release mechanisms on the bars.
- Locations of Registered Sex Offenders disclosure. California law requires real estate contracts to contain the following clause:

  Notice: The California Department of Justice, sheriff's departments, police departments serving jurisdictions of 200,000 or more and many other local law enforcement authorities maintain for public access a data base of the locations of persons required to register pursuant to paragraph (1) of subdivision (a) of Section 290.4 of the Penal Code. The data base is updated on a quarterly basis and a source of information about the presence of these individuals in any neighborhood. The Department of Justice also maintains a Sex Offender Identification Line through which inquiries about individuals may be made. This is a "900" telephone service. Callers must have specific information about individuals they are checking. Information regarding neighborhoods is not available through the "900" telephone service.

■ **Seller Financing Disclosure. If the loan does not qualify for federal disclosure under RESPA or the Truth in Lending Act, California requires a seller financing disclosure which includes comprehensive information about the financing, cautions applicable to certain types of financing, and suggestions of procedures which will protect the parties during the term of the financing. The disclosures include:**

• identification of the note, or credit, or security document and the property which is or will become the security;
• a copy of the note, or credit, or security document, or a description of the terms of these documents;
• the terms and conditions of each encumbrance recorded against the property which shall remain as a lien or is an anticipated lien which will be senior to the financing being arranged;
• a warning about the hazards and potential difficulty of refinancing and, if the existing financing or the financing being arranged involves a balloon payment, the amount and due date of the balloon payment and a warning that new financing may not be available;
• an explanation of the possible effects of an increase in the amount owed due to negative amortization as a result of any variable or adjustable-rate financing being arranged;
• if the financing involves an all-inclusive trust deed (AITD), a statement of the possible penalties, discounts, responsibilities, and rights of parties to the transaction with respect to acceleration and/or prepayment of a prior encumbrance as the result of the creation and/or refinancing of the AITD;
• if the financing involves an AITD or a real property sales contract, a statement identifying the party to whom payments will be made and to whom such payments will be forwarded, and if the party receiving and forwarding the payments is not a neutral third party, a warning that the principals may wish to designate a neutral third party;
• a complete disclosure about the prospective buyer, including credit and employment information along with a statement that the disclosure is not a representation of the credit worthiness of the prospective buyer; or, a statement that no representation regarding the credit worthiness of the prospective buyer is being made;
• a warning regarding possible limitations on the seller's ability, in the event of foreclosure, to recover proceeds of the sale financed (Code of Civil Procedure Section 580b);

• a statement recommending loss payee clauses be added to the property insurance policy to protect the seller's interest (e.g., Board of Fire Underwriters' Endorsement No. B.F.U. 438) and advising of the existence or availability of services which will notify the seller if the property taxes are not paid;
• a statement suggesting or acknowledging that the seller should file or has filed a request for notice of delinquency (Civil Code Section 2924e) and a request for notice of default (Civil Code Section 2924b) in case the buyer fails to pay liens senior to the financing being arranged;
• a statement that a title insurance policy has been or will be obtained and furnished to the buyer and seller insuring their respective interests, or that the buyer and seller should each obtain title insurance coverage;
• a disclosure whether the security documents for the financing being arranged have been or will be recorded, and what might occur if the documents are not recorded; and,
• information as to whether the buyer is to receive any "cash back" from the sale, including the amount, source, and purpose of the cash refund.
Source: California Department of Real Estate "Disclosures in Real Property Transactions."

Other states have additional Consumer Credit laws that are also applicable. For example, Indiana's Consumer Credit Act defines a "lender" as anyone who extends credit. The law requires:

- an interest rate less than 21%
- loan origination fee of not more than 2%
- returned check fee cannot exceed $20
- late fee cannot exceed $5 and can only be applied if payment is more than 10 days late.

A Word on Late Fees

Late fees are small charges designed to help you recover the costs associated with processing a late payment. When creating your own contract, it's tempting to use high late fees or an escalating structure ($x per day late, etc) as an incentive for your borrower to send his or her payments on time. Don't do it! Not only are such fees capped in most states, you run the risk of creating a reverse mortgage situation where the principle balance actually increases over time – a predatory lending practice under increasing surveillance by the regulatory agencies. Your note doesn't need a "creative" late fee clause to ensure that your borrower pays the mortgage as foreclosure should be incentive enough!

Escrow Accounts

_____   (a) Escrow Not Required: Buyer shall furnish Seller annually, before the taxes become delinquent, evidence that all taxes on the Property have been paid. Buyer shall furnish Seller annually evidence of paid-up casualty insurance naming Seller as an additional loss payee.

(b) Escrow Required: With each installment Buyer shall deposit with Seller in escrow a pro rata part of the estimated annual ad valorem taxes and casualty insurance premiums for the Property. Buyer shall pay any deficiency within 30 days after notice from Seller. Buyer's failure to pay the deficiency constitutes a default under the security instrument. Buyer is not required to deposit any escrow payments for taxes and insurance that are deposited with a superior lienholder. The casualty insurance must name Seller as an additional loss payee.

You've seen the standard contract language on Escrow or Impound accounts, perhaps in a Seller Financing Addendum (see above), but when should you require Escrow and how should you manage the account? In this section, we'll discuss the unique requirements of maintaining a real estate Escrow account.

Why collect Escrow? – Escrow accounts are designed to protect the lender's investment in the property by ensuring that funds are available for the borrower to pay property taxes and insurance premiums. Most institutional lenders require Escrow accounts when the borrower puts down less than 20%, but you have the right to contract for an escrow account regardless of the down payment amount. Lenders like Escrow because it spreads out the annual tax bill over the course of a year, eliminating the surprise of one big bill. If you choose to give your borrower the option of handling their own payments, your buyer must furnish annual proof that the payment was made.

Legal limits – The law is very specific in setting limits on the amount that the lender may collect. The lender may require a monthly payment of 1/12 of the total amount of estimated taxes, insurance premiums, and other charges reasonably anticipated to be paid. In addition, the lender may collect an additional balance of not more than 1/6 of the estimated annual payments as a cushion. If the lender determines there will be or is a deficiency in the escrow accounts, the law permits the lender to require additional monthly deposits to avoid or eliminate the deficiency.

Interest on Escrow accounts – Some states, such as New York and Maine, require the quarterly payment of interest to the borrower on escrow balances. Currently, about a quarter of the states require interest to be paid on escrow accounts.

Other Legal Issues – Escrow accounts are covered under section 10 of RESPA. RESPA requires anyone holding an escrow account to submit an annual report to the borrower itemizing "the amount of the borrower's current monthly payment, the portion of the monthly payment being placed in the escrow account, the total amount paid into the escrow account during the period, the total amount paid out of the escrow account during the period for taxes, insurance premiums, and other charges (as separately identified), and the balance in the escrow account at the conclusion of the period."

Note that RESPA holds the lender responsible for payment of any items for which funds are held in escrow. If the lender is assessed a late penalty on property taxes, for example, they may not deduct that fee from the escrow balance nor pass that fee on to the borrower.

IRS 1098 Reporting Requirements

To help consumers accurately deduct mortgage interest from their taxes, the IRS requires most lenders to submit annual 1098 forms to both the agency and the borrower. If you're required to submit this form, accurate record keeping is essential.

Does this apply to me? – The IRS says that you should file a 1098 under the following circumstances:

> If you are engaged in a trade or business and, in the course of such trade or business, you receive from an individual $600 or more of mortgage interest on any one mortgage during the calendar year.

You are not required to file this form if the interest is not received in the course of your trade or business. For example, you hold the mortgage on your former personal residence. The buyer makes mortgage payments to you. You are not required to file Form 1098. **Not in the lending business.**

If you receive $600 or more of mortgage interest in the course of your trade or business, you are subject to the requirement to file Form 1098, even if you are not in the business of lending money. For example, if you are a real estate developer and you provide financing to an individual to buy a home in your subdivision, and that home is security for the financing, you are subject to this reporting requirement. However, if you are a physician not engaged in any other business and you lend money to an individual to buy your home, you are not subject to this reporting requirement because you did not receive the interest in the course of your trade or business as a physician.

If you aren't sure whether you should file the 1098 or not, it's generally better to err on the side of caution and file the form. For the copy you send to the IRS, you also need to send along a form 1096 which is the Annual Summary of paper forms submitted to the agency.

Organizing Your Portfolio

Accurate record keeping is essential for anyone holding a real estate note. As we've discussed thus far, there are a variety of legal housekeeping issues that require you to keep a good handle on the exact status of your note. Keeping accurate financial records and pay history will be of immeasurable value in the long run if your buyer defaults. At a minimum, you should keep a ledger of all your payments either in paper form or in a computer spreadsheet. Getting your system setup and organized can be a bit of a chore though. For that reason, I highly recommend using a note servicing program to maintain your records. I've used NoteSmith for over 10 years now to manage our portfolio and I can tell you that having a computer program that keeps up with the nitty-gritty details of a note quickly pays for itself. NoteSmith allows you to enter the particulars of your note, process payments, calculate late fees, print payment coupons, as well as generate the required annual reports I mentioned earlier. The package also has a variety of form letters that allow you to easily send out a letter when your borrower is late, for example. We recommend this program over the other servicing packages out there because of it's low cost for an individual note holder. The software is affordable enough for someone with just one note, yet powerful enough for someone with a portfolio of 500. For more information on NoteSmith, including a downloadable PowerPoint demo, visit their website at notesmith.com.

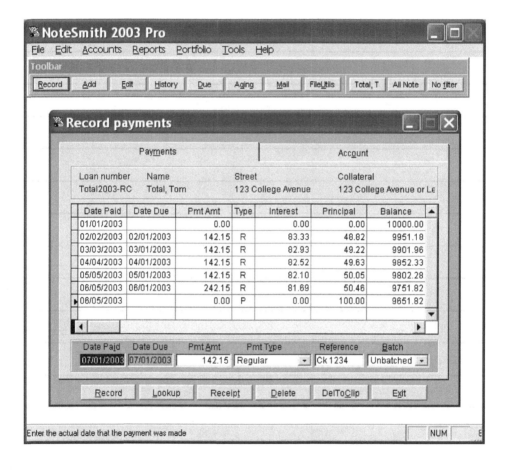

NOTES

Part iii
CONDITIONS LEADING
TO DEFAULT

P&I Delinquency – By far, most defaults are the result of your borrower's failure to make the scheduled Principal and Interest payments. Most loan agreements hold that regular payments are due "on or before" a certain date, but usually a grace period of around 10 days is allowed in which to receive the payment. A late payment charge is typically applied if the payment arrives outside of the grace period. An occasional late payment isn't necessarily something to worry about, but if your borrower consistently pays late or is over 30 days overdue, you may want to consider the loan in default.

Unpaid Property Taxes – A borrower may also default due to failure to pay annual property taxes. This condition represents a significant risk to you as the borrower, because if the property taxes are not paid, the taxing jurisdiction has the right to impose a lien which may assume a higher priority over your position as primary lienholder. If you are unaware of the property tax delinquency, the property may be sold for taxes, thus eliminating your safe lien position. Therefore, all real estate contracts have a clause stipulating that property taxes are to be paid by the borrower on the date required. If the borrower does not comply, you would be notified by the county treasurer, the loan would default and may be accelerated.

No Hazard Insurance – Most real estate agreements also require the borrower to maintain hazard insurance premiums to ensure that your security interest in the property is maintained. Typically, the borrower must submit copies of the paid insurance invoice to you to verify that coverage is in effect. You should be named on the insurance policy as coinsured so that in the event of a problem, your interest position in the property is secured. If the borrower fails to make the required insurance payments, the loan would default and may be accelerated.

Other Liens – Defaults may also occur if the borrower allows other liens that have priority over your loan to vest in the property. Such liens include non-payment of state or federal income tax. In some areas, mechanics' liens (usually a junior lien) may also take priority over the loan. In these instances, it is appropriate to consider the loan in default and to pursue any legal remedies to protect your investment in the property.

Poor Property Management – Real estate loans may also default through a clause in the contract that covers the borrower's responsibility to keep the property in good condition that will not diminish the security value you have invested in the property.

Immediately upon the occurrence of default as mentioned above, it is imperative that the lender make contact with the borrower. *Under these circumstances, time is not on your side!*

Common Sense Collection Calls

One of the best ways to avoid a default by the borrower is through a clear line of communication over the phone. As long as you communicate with the borrower and the borrower feels that he can communicate with you, the chances of a mutually successful resolution are greatly enhanced. Collection calls are a delicate art form, with each situation presenting a unique challenge as to discovering the borrowers motivations and intentions and ultimately how best to deal with the situation. It's the old double edged sword analogy; as a lender, you cannot give the impression that you are soft, that you will do nothing if the borrower consistently pays 25 days late or gets behind several payments and then only sends one payment, or they get it in their mind that you will not go through with foreclosure when you say that you will. However, on the other side of the sword, if you are too aggressive and sound too threatening and give the impression that the borrower has no options and you make demands that they cannot fulfill, the likely outcome is that they will simply give up and you will never hear from them again. You must be polite to keep the communication lines open and give the borrower a glimmer of hope while being firm and as unambiguous as possible.

The Importance of Collecting on Your Note – A poor pay history on a seller financed note is just as damaging to the value of the note as poor property management or any other inherent deficiency that may exist. In order for your note to hold it's value, you must assure that the borrower makes timely payments as agreed in your contract. Once a payment has been missed or a chronic delinquent payment history is produced, the value of your note may drop up to twenty percent or more! An investor will always be willing to pay more for cash flows with excellent pay histories. The pay history you provide to the investor can mean the difference of hundred or even thousand of dollars on the sale of your note. Of course, even if you never sell your note, establishing an excellent pay history is a good practice. Dealing with late payments is a real hassle that can be quite expensive!

Establishing Payment Expectations – While the chance of your borrower being late or missing a monthly payment is probably fairly predictable based on their credit report, even those with good credit run into occasional difficulty. One of the best ways to avoid a default by the borrower is to have pre-established payment expectations at the closing. Before the closing of your loan, you'll want to discuss with the borrower a favorable due date. If you are closing your loan through a title company, make sure that they are also aware of this request. This allows your buyer to take ownership in their repayment responsibility and open up the lines of communication with them. For example, if your note calls for the payment to be due on the 25th of the month and the borrower gets paid on the 1st and 15th of the month, they may have problems getting the payment to you on time. A better due date would be one closer to their payroll date, say on the 5th.

Permanent Corrective Action – Once you have established payment expectations with your borrower, it will be easier to establish "PCA" in the case of a default. PCA stands for Permanent Corrective Action and is basically an established agreed upon action that will be taken by

> **DID YOU KNOW?**
> Once a customer becomes 60 days past due, you only have a 30 percent chance of bringing it current. Establishing PCA on the *first* default is extremely important!

the borrower and you to bring the loan current. For example, let's assume your borrower is two payments past due and you have called and written the customer several times without results. You decide to make an outside call to go see the customer, you find him at home, and he promises to make you one payment. Because it was easier for you and you did not want to confront the borrower, you accepted one payment. Consequently, the next month he pays you on time, but your customer is still one monthly payment past due. You have failed to perform permanent corrective action.

When you talked to your borrower and he promised one payment, you should have immediately made arrangements for the past due payment. For example, if you had arranged for the customer to make a payment and a half now and a payment and half on the next due day, he would be have been current on the next due date. Again, the expectation of keeping the account current would have been reinforced with the customer. By accepting one payment when your customer is two payments past due, you create a "rolling" 30-day account and have just reduced the value of your note.

Collection Schedule – There are an almost endless number reasons a borrower may default on his or her seller-financed note, many of which have been discussed in this book. As soon as a borrower defaults, it is vital that you open communications with them and learn why they have defaulted. You must garner as much information as possible to determine what PCA should be taken. We recommend that you have a regimented collection process that is adhered to regularly. The longer you wait to contact the customer the higher the chance you have **not** collecting the payment. Once a borrower defaults, he or she may be embarrassed to talk with you and might try to hide from you. It's your responsibility to open lines of communication with the payor at once.

The following is a recommended schedule for you to follow to assure that your customers pay on time. We have placed examples of these letters in Appendix B.

5 days delinquent	Reminder Letter
10 days delinquent	First Collection Letter
15 days delinquent	Phone Call with Second Letter
20 days delinquent	Phone Call with Third Letter
30 days delinquent	Demand Letter and visit to property*
30 plus days delinquent	Refer to Attorney for Action

* If possible, we recommend making an outside call to visit your borrower and discuss their reasons for not making payments no later than 30 days past due. If you live in another town, you might consider hiring a realtor to drive by the property to inform you of its' condition. Red flags include deterioration of the property or if the property looks vacant.

Telephone Collection Calls – Always be professional, regardless of what anyone tells you. It is never in your best interest to be anything less that courteous and polite. Yelling, screaming, and/or threatening the borrower are very ineffective methods yielding poor results and could land you in a courtroom for harassment or similar charges. Being firm while maintaining your composure and speaking in a clear, calm voice is the best way to exude control over any situation.

Making a successful collection call is usually the culmination of experience, planning and forethought. Also remember that collection calls are a great opportunity for the lender to not only collect a payment but also update their database as to the borrower's status, such as address, phone number, cell phone number, pager number, employment status, tax and insurance information, etc. One way to give the borrower the impression that you as a lender are always on top of the situation is to consistently communicate as soon as the loan becomes delinquent, and when you speak with the borrower, remember to have all of the account information at your disposal. *This lets the borrower know that you are extremely organized and watching his account like a hawk!*

When making a collection call, always ask open-ended questions. This way you are helping the customer to take ownership in making their payments on time. I like to involve the customer in reaching solutions. For example,. When I need to discipline one of my boys, I employ the tactic of asking him what he thinks would be an appropriate solution to the problem. Often times, the solution he proposes is much harsher than I had in mind. This aspect of human nature can apply to the collection call. If the borrower's solution is harsher than I feel comfortable with, I'm able to propose a more lenient solution which builds even greater rapport and trust with my borrower. Always remember that your borrower originally qualified for your loan, so you need to ask yourself, "What has happened in my customer's life to make them unable to pay on time?"

Keeping Good Pay Histories – Once you have established excellent pay histories with your customers, it is just as important to have these histories documented. You might consider using a computer program to keep track of your pay histories or a paper system if that better suits your style. The payment and collection history gives you a road map of where the account has been. If you decide to later sell your note, providing the investor with a documented pay history will add considerable value to the note.

Skip-Tracing – Skip-tracing is the art and science of finding someone

who has "skipped out" on their obligations. If your borrower defaults on
the property and doesn't leave a calling card, you'll need to track them
down in order to pursue appropriate collection methods. You can hire a
professional skip tracer (private investigators usually do this type of work)
who can track down your borrower, for a fee. If you'd like to look for them
yourself, there are a variety of methods that you can employ. The first
place you would want to check would be to pull out the references he or
she gave you on their credit application. Call each of them, including the
last known employer and any family members, and ask for any information
they can give you on your borrower's whereabouts. If you can keep the
conversation friendly and non-threatening, you'll generally have better
results in convincing folks to help you. You might call the credit card
companies listed on his or her credit report. Many have full-time skip
tracing departments that can provide you with the new contact
information. The public record sources we mentioned in Section I would
also be helpful in tracking down your borrower's new contact information.
If you can pay a personal visit to the property, you might be able to talk to
the neighbors to see if they might have any clues. For example, someone
might be able to tell you what company they used to haul their stuff away
if they saw the van on moving day. You could then try to contact that
company to see where they delivered the furniture. The idea is to find as
much information as you can to try to put together a picture of where your
borrower might be hiding out.

Fair Debt Collection Practices Act

The Fair Debt Collection Practices Act was enacted to protect consumers
from abuses by collection agencies and other debt collectors who harass
and intimidate consumers. There are many technical requirements that
debt collectors must follow under the FDCPA, including limiting contacts
with the debtor, giving the debtor notice that the contact is an effort to
collect a debt and that information obtained may be used against the debtor
and, most importantly, allowing the debtor to request and obtain
verification of the claimed debt and an opportunity to dispute the creditor's
records. It is important to note that creditors are excluded from the Fair
Debt Collection Practices Act and therefore cannot be held accountable
under the act. Under this law, a "Creditor" is not considered a "Debt
Collector" unless:

*creditors, in the process of collecting their own debts, use any
name other than their own which would indicate that a third
person is collecting or attempting to collect such debts.*

*Creditors that use a different name to collect debts become Debt
Collectors and thus must adhere to the FDCPA.*

As a real estate note holder, if you are attempting to collect your own debts
under your own name, the FDCPA does not apply to you. However, if you
turn over your debt collection efforts to a collection agency, the debt
collector you hire must follow all aspects of the Act. The full-text of the
FDCPA may be viewed online at
http://www.ftc.gov/os/statutes/fdcpa/fdcpact.htm. Also, please be aware
that the FDCPA only defines the *minimum* standards – many states have
enacted their own debt collection acts that may apply.

Alternatives to Foreclosure

In a recent study on industry foreclosure practices, it was shown that most
lenders preferred to exercise all other options prior to foreclosure. During
the 1980's, defaults on FHA
loans had risen to the point
where the organization was
holding about 110,000 non-
performing loans on single
family dwellings. In 1994,
Congress ordered the FHA
to divest itself of these
properties and sell them at
public auction. These non-

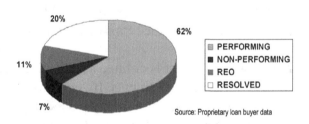

Figure 3: HUD Foreclosure status after 1 year

performing loans were sold mostly to large loan buyers seeking to develop
a portfolio of performing notes. The study sought to determine the status
of the loans after the purchase by these private firms. After less than two
years, the study found that 82% of the loans were still owned by the
original buyers with 62% having been rehabilitated into performing loans,
and 20% categorized as non-performing (see figure 3). Of the 18% of
loans that were no longer in the possession of the private buyer, 7% were
paid-off, while only 11% were foreclosed upon. When you consider that
these stats refer to "problem loans," it's remarkable how few of these

loans entered into foreclosure.

Final foreclosure is avoided whenever possible. Foreclosure sales are known as an investor's paradise for the simple reason that homes sold at auction rarely approach the true market value of the property. If your borrower has little equity in the home, the odds that you are able to recover the full amount of the loan are greatly reduced. For that reason, it is usually advisable to consider alternatives to foreclosure. **Workouts** are the term given to agreements between a borrower and lender to avoid foreclosure and can take a variety of forms.

Forbearance – Also known as a moratorium, these workouts are an attempt to help a borrower through a difficult financial period by offering to reduce or postpone the payments on the note for a set period of time. If your borrower has lost his or her job, for example, you might consider offering a forbearance to allow the borrower a chance to find new employment. You may choose to waive a portion of the payment (usually the principal amount) and just charge the interest during the forbearance. Alternatively, you might waive the entire payment amount and add it to the balance owed when the forbearance is complete. Usually, a condition of forbearance requires the borrower to add money to the regular payments once the loan is restated. If this would cause an additional hardship on your borrower, you might choose to add the amount due to the end of the note, thus extending the terms of the note (or as a final balloon payment).

Recasting – A recast is defined as adjusting the terms of a loan agreement in light of new developments. If your borrower's financial problems could be mitigated by a lower monthly payment, you might choose to restructure the note into a longer term period, allowing the borrower to repay the amount borrowed over a longer period of time. For example, if your borrower is in year 5 of a 15 year $100,000 loan at 8% interest, his or her monthly payments are $955.65 with a balance due of $78,766. You could take that balance due and restructure the loan (perhaps at a higher interest rate given the potential default) over a 30 year period, giving your borrower a new monthly payment of 691.23 (assuming new rate of 10%). Your borrower has over $250 more each month for expenses and your investment in the property remains protected.

Government Assistance – In some cases, especially in the event of disaster, mortgage payment assistance may be available from federal, state and/or local government. Should your borrower ask, you might want to direct them to the following sources:

> FEMA/U.S. Small Business Administration at 1-800-462-9029
> County Emergency Assistance Programs/Human Service Division
> Homeless Prevention Program Funds
> Other Supplemental Resources May Include:
>> Energy or Utility Assistance Program Funds
>> Federal Earned Income Tax Credit
>> Food Stamps

Finally, if your borrower approaches you with financial problems, don't be too quick in dismissing them. Keep in mind that there are many debt companies out there that are more than happy to "help" your borrowers with their credit problems, often with little regard to your interest in the property. These firms advertise heavily in the newspapers and on late night television, presenting an image of escaping all debt without recourse. If your borrower comes to you for advice, there are a few sound financial planning tips that you can give them. First, you should always encourage your borrower to pay your loan first, since secured loans aren't covered under a Chapter 7 bankruptcy. Debt consolidation loans should be avoided since they create a second mortgage that can cause your borrower to lose the house if they default on the new payment. Credit card companies love these types of solutions because they take unsecured consumer debt and turn them into debt that is secured by the house. I would also advise a borrower to be wary of consumer credit services. These services are funded by the credit card companies and therefore often do not have the best interests of the borrower at heart. The services often structure an unreasonable payoff plan that dooms it to failure, meaning money that should go to paying the mortgage gets diverted to paying the credit card companies. The idea here is not to encourage your borrower to default on his or her credit cards, but to simply make sure they understand the financial realities of their debt. Failure to pay credit cards may result in a negative credit report and debt collection efforts. Failure to pay on the house **will** result in foreclosure!

What to Expect When Your Loan Enters Default

When your borrower runs behind in his or her obligations on the note and mortgage, and all efforts to salvage the loan through collection calls, workout agreements and/or restructuring have failed, there are several possible scenarios for which you need to prepare: Bankruptcy, Foreclosure, Surrender of the Deed to the note holder, or presale of the property prior to Foreclosure are among the likely examples of how your loan may end up after it has become seriously delinquent. The first two options are unilateral decisions by the borrower while the latter pair allow you and the borrower to work together to reach a workable solution. Let's look at each in turn.

Bankruptcy - While bankruptcy should be the course of last resort for your borrower, the thought of "erasing"debt, along with aggressive advertising on the part of bankruptcy lawyers, often causes borrowers to consider defaulting before pursuing other options. Bankruptcy is defined as the legal process by which a debtor hands over his assets to the bankruptcy court and is relieved of the future obligation to repay his or her unsecured debts. The important phrase to note here is *unsecured debts*. For your purposes as a note holder, bankruptcy is usually a delaying action, meaning that it doesn't resolve the default on the mortgage. Under a Chapter 7 liquidation bankruptcy, all non-exempt assets are liquidated as full payment for the debt. Under a Chapter 13 reorganization, a repayment plan is created with the help of a court appointed trustee to repay some or all of the debt in a set period (usually 3-5 years).

As a mortgage holder, you more than likely represent the borrower's greatest financial liability. If the borrower has demonstrated a willingness to work with you to keep the home, bankruptcy proceedings need not affect you negatively. In fact, in many instances, bankruptcy (especially the reorganization varieties) may actually help your borrower make his or her monthly payments, as less household funds are diverted to pay various consumer debt. However, if the borrower is in default on your note, it's important to understand that bankruptcy proceedings do change your options for collection. When a bankruptcy gets filed, an automatic stay on litigation such as foreclosures

> **DID YOU KNOW?**
>
> According to Fannie Mae, of every 100 borrowers who are 30 days late on their mortgages, only 11 will miss a second payment; only 4 will go on to miss a third payment; and fewer than 2 will go into foreclosure.

is issued (11 U.S.C. 362). To get around the stay you must go into court and ask the bankruptcy judge for a **relief from stay**. Some of the reasons a relief from stay may be granted include:

- Borrower defaults on scheduled Chapter 13 or Chapter 11 payments.
- Borrower fails to file a reorganization plan or other required documents on time.
- Borrower's income is insufficient to execute a reorganization plan within the court's guidelines.
- The asset in question will not be needed to reorganize.
- The value of the asset is rapidly eroding.
- Borrower files a chapter 7.

Usually in the case of a mortgage holder, your argument for a relief from stay might include showing that the creditor's interest in particular property is not "adequately protected," or showing that the debtor has little/no equity in the property. You can often get relief from the stay to foreclose on property in which the borrower has no equity or where the property is not insured. In cases where the "equity cushion" (the difference between the amount owed you and the value of the property) is small, the borrower may have to make "adequate protection payments" to the note holder to preserve the equity cushion for your benefit as a condition of the stay remaining in effect. In some cases, you may want relief from stay to pursue the borrower's insurance coverage. Such relief is generally granted if you agree to limit the collection of the judgment to the insurance.

Note that when relief from stay is granted, it does not remove the property from the estate or grant the note holder ownership of the property. It simply removes the stay and restores your rights under state law and allows you to enforce those rights to the extent that the relief from stay order permits. In other words, a relief from stay order simply allows you to take whatever action is normally allowed outside of bankruptcy.

So what steps should you take when you receive a notice of bankruptcy from the court on your borrower? The first step is to **immediately cease all collection efforts**. As mentioned above, you must get a court-ordered relief from stay before you can pursue independent collection efforts. Secondly, you will want to **file a claim** with the court clerk. A sample claim form is included in Appendix B or can be downloaded at www.uscourts.gov/FormsAndFees.aspx. The court will need a copy of your real estate note. Thirdly, you will want to monitor the progress of the proceedings. If you aren't happy with the borrower's repayment schedules or if you believe that he or she is hiding assets, contact the trustee and let them know anything you can that will help them recover money for the estate. Your claim is secured by the real estate, but in the event that the bankruptcy sale doesn't pay off the mortgage in full, you'll want the pool of available funds to be an accurate record of the borrower's true financial situation.

Foreclosure - Earlier I mentioned that Bankruptcy and Foreclosure are both default options made unilaterally by the borrower. I include Foreclosure in that category because as the note holder's course of last resort, it only occurs due to borrower inaction; namely, a decision on the part of the borrower not to explore one of the dozens of foreclosure alternatives available to him or her.

Judicial Foreclosure – The foreclosure process varies from state to state. Here is a general course of events for those states that employ judicial foreclosure - just keep in mind that some of the specifics may be different for your particular state.

<u>Pre-Foreclosure</u>

1.   Customer misses mortgage payment.
2.   Late notice send by mortgage holder
3.   Customer misses additional payments.
4.   Mortgage holder attempts in writing and by phone to contact customer and resolve situation.
5.   No arrangements are agreed upon and customer continues to miss payments.
6.   Mortgage holder issues demand for payment under the note in full, based on the acceleration clause. Most notes contain language which basically says if the borrower fails to pay under the terms of the note with monthly payments as promised you can accelerate the note, meaning that the full amount is due on demand. At this point, the borrower legally owes the full balance of the mortgage plus back interest, plus late charges, plus legal fees all at once. Note that a few states (e.g. Mississippi) allow the borrower to disregard an acceleration clause by bringing the note current under the original

terms at anytime in the foreclosure process. [If a note reaches this stage and the borrower wishes to make arrangements, you would typically restructure the mortgage to include all fees, etc. rather than allow the borrower to continue with the previous arrangements.]

7.　　No payments or arrangements acceptable to the bank are made.

Formal Legal Foreclosure Process

1.　　Mortgage holder sends by sheriff or by certified mail Notice of Intent to Foreclose[1].
2.　　Mortgage holder begins action in the court system to foreclose.
3.　　Legal notices as required by law begin to be published in local papers.
4.　　No payment or settlement arrangements are made with the mortgage holder.
5.　　Notice and waiting periods expire.
6.　　Court holds hearing regarding mortgage holder claim.
7.　　Court issues order allowing foreclosure
8.　　Legal notice of actual foreclosure sale and advertisements published in local papers.
9.　　No payment arrangements or settlements reached with the mortgage holder.
10.　　House sold at auction to highest bidder.

As you can see from the flowchart above, there are numerous points in the process where your borrower can turn the ship around and stop the foreclosure process. It isn't until the gavel is struck at auction that the borrower is out of luck and even in those extreme instances, deals can be structured given a motivated borrower.

Power-of-Sale Foreclosures – If you are in a state that uses deeds of trust rather than mortgages, your note should contain a power-of-sale option. Under this plan, the lender or the trustee has the right to sell the property upon default without having to go through the expense and hassle of a judicial foreclosure. In the event that your borrower defaults on the loan, you simply notify the trustee of the default and instruct them to begin the

---

[1]See Appendix B for a sample form.

sale process. Typically, notice of the default is recorded in the courthouse within the designated time period to give notice of the impending sale to the general public. This official recording is accompanied by newspaper announcements that state the total amount due and the date of the sale. If your state allows for a redemption period, the borrower (or any junior lienholder) may cure the default by making up the delinquent payments, along with interest and all other expenses. If the payments aren't made, however, the property is placed up for auction and the title goes to the successful bidder.

Deficiency Judgements – At the foreclosure auction, you as the lender would typically make the opening bid in the amount of the total due, along with interest and any other expenses due you. If anyone bids an amount above the first mortgage, the excess funds are distributed first to any junior lienholders (in order of priority), with any remaining funds going to the defaulted borrower. In some states, if you foreclose on your borrower and the amount of the sale doesn't cover the balance due on the mortgage, you can sue for a deficiency judgment against the borrower. This amount of the judgement is the difference between the balance owed on the mortgage and the amount recovered at the foreclosure sale. Some states (e.g. Texas) now limit deficiency judgments to the difference between fair market value and the balance owed on the loan. The deficiency judgment becomes an unsecured debt owed to you by the borrower and can be pursued via normal debt collection avenues. When you are awarded a deficiency judgment from the court, you are also given an unsecured blanket lien which can be attached to any property currently owned or acquired in the future by the borrower. In most cases, the defaulting borrower doesn't have any other assets (otherwise, they would have used them to save their house), so deficiency judgments are usually very difficult to collect. Unfortunately, a dishonest borrower can easily avoid a deficiency judgment by ensuring that they don't own any property in their own name. Many states have eliminated, or are considering eliminating, deficiency judgements, so be sure to check your local laws before pursuing a course of action that relies on securing a deficiency judgment.

Surrender of Deed – Sometimes called "deed in lieu of foreclosure," this type of default occurs when the borrower transfers the deed to the lender in exchange for cancellation of the remaining debt. As a lender, you are under no obligation to accept a surrender of deed agreement, but if the circumstances allow, it may be an attractive alternative to the expense of judicial foreclosure. If your property has maintained market value or if your borrower has built up sufficient equity to cover your expenses in reselling the property, you would simply cancel the existing loan and place the property back on the market. One danger in surrender of deed transactions is that any junior liens that the borrower has placed on the property may remain in effect. So, as a rule of thumb, you cannot accept a "deed in lieu" with junior liens in place without first satisfying those liens. We recommend an extensive title search to ensure that you don't inherit any unknown encumbrances.

Note that it is important to establish if the borrower will later file bankruptcy because a surrender of deed transaction could possibly be set aside if the transfer was a preference or fraudulent transfer under the Bankruptcy Code. A preference is defined in Section 547 (b) of the Bankruptcy Code as a transfer of property of the debtor, to or for the benefit of a creditor, for or on account of an antecedent debt, made while the debtor was insolvent, within 90 days before bankruptcy (or one year if the creditor was an insider), which enables the creditor to receive more than the creditor would receive under a Chapter 7 distribution - or more than the lender's secured claim.

Because the surrender of deed may not extinguish subordinate liens on the property, you may want to consider what is typically termed a **friendly foreclosure**. A friendly foreclosure is nothing more than a regular foreclosure where the borrower agrees not to contest the foreclosure or declare bankruptcy in exchange for full or partial forgiveness of any remaining debt.

By conducting a friendly foreclosure, you're able to advertise the foreclosure sale as required by the deed and also market the property via the use of a professional auctioneer. Taking title to the property via surrender of deed will expedite the transfer of title to you, however, finding a buyer and selling the property will require additional time and expense. Use of the friendly foreclosure will permit you to conduct the foreclosure against the property and purge the real estate of any subordinate liens, while also allowing the opportunity to aggressively market the property in an effort to maximize the price at the foreclosure sale.

Presale of Property – Also known as **short sales**, this default method is sometimes used when the borrower wants to avoid foreclosure and owes more than the current market value of the home. You and the borrower can negotiate a deal if you're willing to accept less than the amount due on the mortgage provided that the borrower can find a buyer for the home. You and the borrower reach an appropriate "workout" amount and the borrower places the home on the market. As a note holder you will want to investigate all other options before agreeing to a reduction in the mortgage amount; however, if other debt collection methods are unlikely to yield the full amount or if you don't wish to pursue foreclosure, short selling the property may allow you to recover a larger portion of your investment than otherwise possible. Sometimes, "a bird in the hand is worth two in the bush;" especially if the subject property is in bad condition or the resale market is slow. If you agree to a short sale, you may want to consider the FHA guidelines for short sales that have become standard practice. Generally, the requirements are: borrower must occupy the home, borrower must be at least three months in arrears, and there must be a documented hardship before this type of sale will be permitted. If your borrower requests a short sale, the following guidelines (variances allowed) are typically used: the appraised value is at least 70% of amount owing, proceeds of the sale should be at least 87% of the value, and the sale must close within 90 days of borrower approval.

Tax Consequences of Default

It is important to remember that when a borrower must utilize the short sale, surrender of deed option, or a foreclosure takes place, the IRS requires all lenders to send a 1099 Income Earnings Statement to all borrowers on the note for any deficiency balance (forgiveness of debt according to the IRS) in excess of $600. This must be reported on the borrower's tax returns as income and taxes may be assessed.

The IRS has ruled that foreclosure of real property, through a trustee's sale, will produce taxable income for the borrower to the extent that the loan balance exceeds the tax basis of the property in the year of sale. Discharge of debt income is ordinary income and therefore taxed at regular rates. The lender must issue a form 1099-C if part of the transaction is considered as income from the discharge of debt. The borrower will have capital gain income in the amount of the excess of the fair market value of the property over its tax basis. For example, assume the borrower is personally liable on the mortgage, the loan balance is $900,000, and the property has a fair market value of $650,000 and tax basis of $600,000. Upon foreclosure through a trustee's sale, the borrower will have $250,000 of discharge of debt income and $50,000 of capital gain income. Deed in lieu of foreclosure transactions should generally produce the same results as a foreclosure transaction. When the borrower undergoes a short sale it should be treated as above, with the sales price being equivalent to the fair market value if the transaction is arms length.

IRS Publication 537 (available online at www.irs.gov or from 1-800-829-3676) outlines the specific tax consequences generated by repossession of an installment sale:

> The rules for the repossession of real property allow you to keep essentially the same adjusted basis in the repossessed property you had before the original sale. You can recover this entire adjusted basis when you resell the property. This, in effect, cancels out the tax treatment that applied to you on the original sale and puts you in the same tax position you were in before that sale.

> Therefore, the total payments you have received from the buyer on the original sale must be considered income to you. You report, as gain on the repossession, any part of the payments you have not yet included in income. These payments are amounts you previously treated as a return of your adjusted basis and excluded from income. However, the total gain you report is limited.

> *Example.* You sold a tract of land in January 2000 for $25,000. You accepted a $5,000 down payment, plus a $20,000 mortgage secured by the property and payable at the rate of $4,000 annually plus interest (9.5%). The payments began on January 1, 2001. Your adjusted basis in the property was $19,000 and you reported the transaction as an installment sale. Your selling expenses were $1,000. You figured your gross profit as follows:

Selling price		$25,000
Minus:		
Adjusted basis	$19,000	
Selling expenses	1,000	20,000
Gross profit		**$ 5,000**

For this sale, the contract price equals the selling price. The gross profit percentage is 20% ($5,000 gross profit ÷ $25,000 contract price).

In 2000, you included $1,000 in income (20% × $5,000 down payment). In 2001, you reported a profit of $800 (20% × $4,000 annual installment). In 2002, the buyer defaulted and you repossessed the property. You paid $500 in legal fees to get your property back. Your taxable gain on the repossession is figured as follows:

1.	Payments received before repossession		$9,000
2.	Minus: Gain reported		1,800
3.	Gain on repossession		$7,200
4.	Gross profit on sale		$5,000
5.	Gain reported (line 2)	$1,800	
6.	Plus: Repossession costs	500 2,300	
7.	Subtract line 6 from line 4		$2,700
8.	**Taxable gain (lesser of line 3 or 7)**		**$2,700**

Selling Your Note

Like any other commodity, real estate notes have a cash value in the marketplace. As you can imagine, a variety of factors determine the value of a note. I mentioned earlier that the value of a note is affected by the down payment, interest rate, payment amount, and term as well as the buyer's credit rating and payment history. The type, condition, and value of the property also impact the value. The tips and techniques discussed in Section ii, Structuring the Sale, will help maximize the value of your note. But even if you created your note without this information, selling your note is still an available option. Please call your note specialist to discuss how much your note is worth.

Let's say that you have sold your home using owner-financing and now collect a monthly payment of $450 from the buyer. You decided to offer owner financing because of the advantages it presents in selling the property: a quicker closing time, the ability to sell to a larger pool of potential buyers, or perhaps conventional financing wasn't available on your property type. But consider this: if you had been able to use conventional financing, you would have received a check from the bank from the sale of the property. Rather than having to wait 30 years to receive your funds, you would be able to take the money and reinvest it in another property or some other type of return, such as your business, kid's education or the like. However, by receiving your large investment $450 at a time, it can be difficult to really use that money to its full potential. In other words, you may discover that those monthly checks are just absorbed into your household income.

What if you are a property developer and have taken back a note to finance the sale of lots in your development, or a rehabber who provides owner-financing on the properties you have fixed up? Seller-financing is a great business strategy because it offers you the ability to turn your properties quickly. The problem with seller-financing vs. conventional financing is that your working capital is now tied up in these properties. However, by working with an experience note buyer, you have all the benefits of seller-financing without having to tie up your funds in notes. Additionally the transaction can be structured as a simultaneous close, allowing you to receive your funds at closing just as in conventional financing. To take another example, let's say that you have structured a lease-purchase agreement with your buyer to allow them time to come up with long term financing. But what happens if you reach the end of the option term and they haven't been able to secure conventional financing? Why not offer seller-financing and then sell the created note? You'll receive the funds you need for future projects and your borrower gets the financing they need to fulfill the dream of home ownership.

Partial Purchases – In addition to an outright purchase of the note, a "partial" purchase can be structured that gives you immediate cash for a set number of payments, after which time the note reverts back to you. If you need to raise a specific amount of capital, a partial allows you to receive exactly the amount that you need without having to cash out the entire note. A partial is one example of how we can work around a less than perfect note. Partial purchases are actually pretty common in the finance world. Banks have been selling loan portions (participations) to each other for over 50 years. It allows the origination lender to sell and recoup a large portion of their cash, which leverages their loans generating a better return.

The easiest way to understand how partials work would be to take a specific example. In the attached graph, we show a typical 30 year loan amortization along with a partial purchase of the first 15 years of payments. Mrs. Smart sold 15 years of her loan. The loan balance at the time of her sale was $88,000, represented by point A on the upper line of the graph. The investor purchased the first 15 years of payments for $72,000 which we'll track on the lower line. Since Mrs. Smart did not sell the entire loan, she still has equity in the loan as shown in the lightly shaded portion of the graph. Notice that as the payments are made, the lower line (investor's entitlement) reduces much quicker than the upper line (entire note entitlement). In other words, Mrs. Smart's equity increases with every payment made (the lightly shaded area gets larger). At the end of the 15 year period (point C), the entitlement due the investor has amortized to zero. The loan balance is still $76,000 and that is the amount that reverts back to Mrs. Smart. At the beginning of the sale, she receives a significant amount of cash for the partial purchase and also collects the remaining $76,000 plus interest at the end of the partial term. At her option, Mrs. Smart could either collect the payments on reassignment or sell that portion of the note. Mrs. Smart is aptly named!

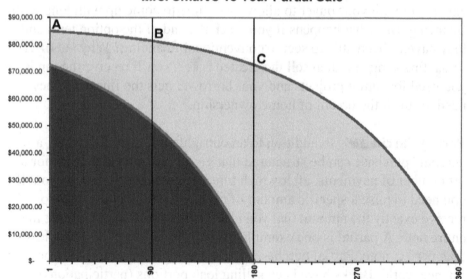

Mrs. Smart's 15 Year Partial Sale

Month	Loan Balance	Entitlement Due Investor
1	$88,000	$72,000
90	$84,000	$51,000
180	$76,000	$0

NOTES

CONCLUSION

Successful seller financing involves making a variety of important decisions. It is my hope that this book prompts you in asking the appropriate questions to structure and service your sale. Know that this book is an ever growing resource and as the seller financing industry changes, we'll change right along with it. If you have any questions about anything that we covered, don't hesitate to contact your note professional.

Appendix A
GLOSSARY OF TERMS

acceleration clause – a common provision of real estate contracts which allows the holder to demand payment in full in the event of a breach of the contract.

addendum – an agreement or list that is added to a contract such as a letter of intent. FHA and VA regulations require that the addendum be added to or incorporated into the sales contract, if it is written prior to the appraisal.

additional insured – an individual, business or organization covered by a policy in addition to the named insured.

ad valorem taxes – real estate taxes on the assessed value of the property.

amortization – repayment of a mortgage debt with periodic payments of both principal and interest, calculated to retire the obligation at the end of a fixed period of time.

annual percentage rate (APR) – defined in section 106 of the federal Truth in Lending Act, which expresses on an annualized basis the charges imposed on the borrower to obtain a loan (defined in the Act as "finance charges"), including interest, discount and other costs.

arm's length transaction – a transaction between a willing buyer and a willing seller with no undue influence imposed on either party and where there is no relationship between the parties except that of the specific transaction.

balloon mortgage – a mortgage with periodic installments of principal and interest that do not fully amortize the loan. The balance of the mortgage is due in a lump sum at a specified date, usually at the end of the term.

carryback financing – an agreement in which the seller takes back a note for part of the purchase price secured by a junior mortgage, wrap-around mortgage or contract for deed.

combined loan-to-value – the principal balance of all mortgages on the property (including second and third trusts) divided by the balance of the property.

commingling – combining funds (such as escrows) into one account that should be accounted for and deposited into separate accounts.

conventional financing – mortgage financing which is not insured or guaranteed by a government agency.

debt-to-income ratio – relationship of a borrower's monthly payment obligation on long-term debts divided by gross monthly income, expressed as a percentage.

deed-in-lieu – a deed given by a borrower to a lender to satisfy a debt and avoid foreclosure.

deed of trust – a type a security instrument in which the borrower conveys title to real property to a third party (trustee) to be hend in trust as security for the lender, with the provision that the trustee shall reconvey the title upon payment of the debt, and, conversely, will sell the land and pay the debt in the event of a default by the borrower.

default – the non-payment of a mortgage or other loan in accordance with the terms as specified in the note.

deficiency judgement – a court order to pay the balance owed on a loan of the proceeds from the sale fo the security are insufficient to pay off the loan.

escrow – an item of value, money or documents, deposited with a third party to be delivered upon the fulfillment of a condition. For example, the deposit by a borrower with the lender of funds to pay taxes and insurance premiums when the become due, or the deposit of funds or documents with an attorney or escrow agent to be disbursed upon the closing of a real estate transaction. In some areas of the country, escrows of taxes and insurance premiums are called **impounds** or **reserves**.

first lien – a lien that gives the holder a security right over all other liens on the encumbered property.

foreclosure – a legal procedure in which a mortgaged property is sold in a legal process to pay the outstanding debt in case of default.

homestead estate – in some states (such as Texas), a statutory exemption which prohibits the attachment or sale of owner-occupied properties to pay the claims of creditors.

judicial foreclosure – type of foreclosure proceeding used in some states that is handled as a civil lawsuit and conducted entirely under the auspices of a court.

lease-purchase – a method of acquiring ownership of real estate through gradual payments under which a lease is substituted for a mortgage obligation. Also referred to as a lease with option to purchase.

lien – a legal hold or claim of a creditor on the property of another as security for a debt. Liens may be against real or personal property.

loan-to-value ratio (LTV) – the ratio of the amount of the loan to the appraised value or sales price of real property, expressed as a percentage.

military indulgence – the protection enacted and provided by the Soldier's and Sailor's Civil Relief Act to a mortgagor who is about to enter or is in the military and whose ability to keep a loan current has been materially affected by military service.

PITI – acronym for the items included in a monthly mortgage payment: principal, interest, taxes and insurance.

power of sale – a provision in a deed of trust or mortgage that empowers a trustee, without court order, to sell property in the event of default by the mortgagor and to apply the proceeds of the sale to satisfy the obligation, the costs of invoking the procedure, and the expenses of the sale.

priority – the order of precedence of liens against the property or assets. Priority is usually established by filing or recording of liens, but may be established by statute or agreement.

private mortgage insurance (PMI) – insurance written by a private company protecting the lender from loss in the event of a borrower defaulting on a mortgage.

redemption period – the time allowed by law in some states during which mortgagors may buy back their foreclosed properties by paying the balance owed on their delinquent mortgages, plus interest and fees. Varies by state from 30 days to 2 years or more.

Regulation Z – regulation written by the Federal Reserve Board which implements the Truth in Lending Act. Requires full written disclosure of the credit portion of a purchase, including the annual percentage rate.

restructure – a loan for which the basic terms, such as interest rate, maturity date, collateral, or guaranty have been modified as a result of actual or anticipated delinquency.

underwriting – the analysis of the risk involved in making a mortgage loan to determine whether the risk is acceptable to the lender. Underwriting involves the evaluation of the property as outlined in the appraisal, and of the borrower's ability and willingness to repay the loan.

Uniform Settlement Statement (HUD-1) – settlement summary form required by RESPA to be used by closing agents.

workout – an alternative to foreclosure for the benefit of the lender and the borrower. Includes loan modifications, short sales and various forms of forbearance.

Appendix B
IMPORTANT FORMS

Form B10 - US Bankruptcy Court Proof of Claim
(http://www.uscourts.gov/bankform/)

FORM B10 (Official Form 10) (4/01)

UNITED STATES BANKRUPTCY COURT _____ DISTRICT OF _____		PROOF OF CLAIM
Name of Debtor	Case Number	

NOTE: This form should not be used to make a claim for an administrative expense arising after the commencement of the case. A "request" for payment of an administrative expense may be filed pursuant to 11 U.S.C. § 503.

Name of Creditor (The person or other entity to whom the debtor owes money or property):	☐ Check box if you are aware that anyone else has filed a proof of claim relating to your claim. Attach copy of statement giving particulars.	
Name and address where notices should be sent:	☐ Check box if you have never received any notices from the bankruptcy court in this case. ☐ Check box if the address differs from the address on the envelope sent to you by the court.	
Telephone number:		THIS SPACE IS FOR COURT USE ONLY
Account or other number by which creditor identifies debtor:	Check here if this claim ☐ replaces ☐ amends a previously filed claim, dated: _____	

1. Basis for Claim
- ☐ Goods sold
- ☐ Services performed
- ☐ Money loaned
- ☐ Personal injury/wrongful death
- ☐ Taxes
- ☐ Other _____

☐ Retiree benefits as defined in 11 U.S.C. § 1114(a)
☐ Wages, salaries, and compensation (fill out below)
Your SS #: _____
Unpaid compensation for services performed
from _____ (date) to _____ (date)

2. Date debt was incurred:

3. If court judgment, date obtained:

4. Total Amount of Claim at Time Case Filed: $ _____
If all or part of your claim is secured or entitled to priority, also complete Item 5 or 6 below.
☐ Check this box if claim includes interest or other charges in addition to the principal amount of the claim. Attach itemized statement of all interest or additional charges.

5. Secured Claim.
☐ Check this box if your claim is secured by collateral (including a right of setoff).
Brief Description of Collateral:
☐ Real Estate ☐ Motor Vehicle ☐ Other _____
Value of Collateral: $ _____
Amount of arrearage and other charges at time case filed included in secured claim, if any: $ _____

6. Unsecured Priority Claim.
☐ Check this box if you have an unsecured priority claim
Amount entitled to priority $ _____
Specify the priority of the claim:
- ☐ Wages, salaries, or commissions (up to $4,650),* earned within 90 days before filing of the bankruptcy petition or cessation of the debtor's business, whichever is earlier - 11 U.S.C. § 507(a)(4).
- ☐ Contributions to an employee benefit plan - 11 U.S.C. § 507(a)(3).
- ☐ Up to $2,100* of deposits toward purchase, lease, or rental of property or services for personal, family, or household use - 11 U.S.C. § 507(a)(6).
- ☐ Alimony, maintenance, or support owed to a spouse, former spouse, or child - 11 U.S.C. § 507(a)(7).
- ☐ Taxes or penalties owed to governmental units - 11 U.S.C. § 507(a)(8).
- ☐ Other - Specify applicable paragraph of 11 U.S.C. § 507(a)(___).
*Amounts are subject to adjustment on 4/1/04 and every 3 years thereafter with respect to cases commenced on or after the date of adjustment.

7. Credits: The amount of all payments on this claim has been credited and deducted for the purpose of making this proof of claim.

8. Supporting Documents: *Attach copies of supporting documents,* such as promissory notes, purchase orders, invoices, itemized statements of running accounts, contracts, court judgments, mortgages, security agreements, and evidence of perfection of lien. DO NOT SEND ORIGINAL DOCUMENTS. If the documents are not available, explain. If the documents are voluminous, attach a summary.

9. Date-Stamped Copy: To receive an acknowledgment of the filing of your claim, enclose a stamped, self-addressed envelope and copy of this proof of claim.

THIS SPACE IS FOR COURT USE ONLY

Date	Sign and print the name and title, if any, of the creditor or other person authorized to file this claim (attach copy of power of attorney, if any).

Penalty for presenting fraudulent claim: Fine of up to $500,000 or imprisonment for up to 5 years, or both. 18 U.S.C. §§ 152 and 3571.

Sample Freddie Mac Universal Loan Application

Uniform Residential Loan Application

This application is designed to be completed by the applicant(s) with the lender's assistance. Applicants should complete this form as "Borrower" or "Co-Borrower", as applicable. Co-Borrower information must also be provided (and the appropriate box checked) when ☐ the income or assets of a person other than the "Borrower" (including the Borrower's spouse) will be used as a basis for loan qualification or ☐ the income or assets of the Borrower's spouse will not be used as a basis for loan qualification, but his or her liabilities must be considered because the Borrower resides in a community property state, the security property is located in a community property state, or the Borrower is relying on other property located in a community property state as a basis for repayment of the loan.

I. TYPE OF MORTGAGE AND TERMS OF LOAN

Mortgage Applied for:	☐ VA ☐ Conventional ☐ Other: ☐ FHA ☐ FmHA		Agency Case Number	Lender Case Number
Amount $	Interest Rate %	No. of Months	Amortization Type: ☐ Fixed Rate ☐ GPM	☐ Other (explain): ☐ ARM (type):

II. PROPERTY INFORMATION AND PURPOSE OF LOAN

Subject Property Address (street, city, state & zip code)		County	No. of Units
Legal Description of Subject Property (attach description if necessary)			Year Built

Purpose of Loan ☐ Purchase ☐ Construction ☐ Other (explain): ☐ Refinance ☐ Construction-Permanent	Property will be: ☐ Primary Residence ☐ Secondary Residence ☐ Investment

Complete this line if construction or construction-permanent loan.

Year Lot Acquired	Original Cost $	Amount Existing Liens $	(a) Present Value of Lot $	(b) Cost of Improvements $	Total (a+b) $

Complete this line if this is a refinance loan.

Year Acquired	Original Cost $	Amount Existing Liens $	Purpose of Refinance	Describe Improvements ☐ made ☐ to be made Cost: $

Title will be held in what Name(s)	Manner in which Title will be held	Estate will be held in: ☐ Fee Simple ☐ Leasehold (show expiration date)
Source of Down Payment, Settlement Charges and/or Subordinate Financing (explain)		

III. BORROWER INFORMATION

Borrower				Co-Borrower			
Borrower's Name (include Jr. or Sr. if applicable)				Co-Borrower's Name (include Jr. or Sr. if applicable)			
Social Security Number	Home Phone (incl. area code)	Age	Yrs. School	Social Security Number	Home Phone (incl. area code)	Age	Yrs. School
☐ Married ☐ Unmarried (include single, divorced, widowed) ☐ Separated		Dependents (not listed by Co-Borrower) no. ages		☐ Married ☐ Unmarried (include single, divorced, widowed) ☐ Separated		Dependents (not listed by Borrower) no. ages	
Present Address (street, city, state, zip code) ☐ Own ☐ Rent No. Yrs.				Present Address (street, city, state, zip code) ☐ Own ☐ Rent No. Yrs.			

(Full form available at http://www.freddiemac.com/sell/forms/index.html)

Bad Check Notice Form

John Doe
5 Hill Street
Madison, Wisconsin 53700

15 March 2013

Ms. Helen Jones
123 International Lane
Boston, Massachusetts 01234

Dear Ms. Jones:

Payment on your Check No._____in the amount of $_____,
tendered to us on _____, 20____, has been dishonored by
your bank. We have verified with your bank that there are still insufficient
funds to pay the check.

Accordingly, we request that you replace this check with a cash (or
certified check) payment.

Unless we receive good funds for said amount within _____ days, we shall
immediately commence appropriate legal action to protect our interest.
Upon receipt of replacement funds we shall return to you the dishonored
check.

Sincerely,

John Doe

Certified Mail, Return Receipt Requested.

Payment Reminder Letter

John Doe
5 Hill Street
Madison, Wisconsin 53700

5 March 2013

Ms. Helen Jones
123 International Lane
Boston, Massachusetts 01234

Dear Ms. Jones:

Subject: Mortgage Payment Reminder

Dear Customer:

This letter is to remind you that you mortgage payment in the amount of
_____ is five days past due. If you are unable to send this in please
call me at (555) 555-1212. Otherwise, we will expect your up to date
payment immediately.

Sincerely,

Notice of Non Payment - Letter # 1

John Doe
5 Hill Street
Madison, Wisconsin 53700

10 March 2013

Ms. Helen Jones
123 International Lane
Boston, Massachusetts 01234

Dear Ms. Jones:

Subject: Notice of Non-Payment

This letter is to notify you that your account is ten (10) days past due in the amount of _____ including late fees in the amount of $_____. If you are unable to make your payment please call me at (555) 555-1212. Otherwise, we will expect you payment in full including late fees within the next three days.

Sincerely,

Notice of Non Payment - Letter # 2

John Doe
5 Hill Street
Madison, Wisconsin 53700

15 March 2012

Ms. Helen Jones
123 International Lane
Boston, Massachusetts 01234

Dear Ms. Jones:

Subject: Notice of Non-Payment

This letter is to notify you that your mortgage payment in the amount of
$_____ and a late fee in the amount of $_____ is fifteen days
past due. We have sent you several letters and have not received a reply,
therefore we will expect payment in full with in three full business days.
Please remit $_____ by _____ to avoid any potential legal action.

If you are unable to comply with this request please call me immediately at
(555) 555-1212.

Sincerely,

Notice of Non Payment - Letter # 3

John Doe
5 Hill Street
Madison, Wisconsin 53700

20 March 2013

Ms. Helen Jones
123 International Lane
Boston, Massachusetts 01234

Dear Ms. Jones:

Subject: Third Notice of Non-Payment

Your mortgage payment in the amount of $_____including late fees
is twenty (20) days past due. We have sent you several letters and have not
received any response. This letter is to notify you if payment is not
received in three days, you account will be referred to our attorney for
collections.

To avoid additional collection expense please remit the above amount
within three days and call me to make arrangements for the April 2004
payment that will be due within the next 10 days.

Sincerely,

Sample Breech Letter (from Fannie Mae)

[Your Company Letterhead]

March 15, 2013

[Borrower Name]
[Borrower Address]
[City, State, Zip]

Re: Property located at _____

Dear [Name of Borrower]:

You have fallen behind on your mortgage payments. You must bring the mortgage current within 30 days of the date of this letter by sending the amount shown below to [Your Company Name] in the form of a money order or certified check.

The total amount due as of [last payment due date] is [$].

You must include any payments or late charges that become due during this 30-day period, along with the amount shown above, to bring your account current. Our acceptance of less than the total amount due does not waive our right to demand the entire balance due under the terms of your mortgage.

If you fail to bring your account current within 30 days of the date of this letter, we will demand the entire balance outstanding under the terms of your mortgage. This amount includes, but is not limited to, the principal, interest, and all other outstanding charges and costs. We will start action to foreclose on the mortgage, which could result in the sale of the property. We may also have the right to seek a judgment against you for any deficiency.

You have the right to bring your account current even after legal action has begun. You also have the right to assert in the foreclosure proceeding the nonexistence of the default or any other defense to our legal action and sale of the property.

We want to work with you to resolve the problem and help you bring your account in good standing. We urge you to contact [name] at [telephone number] who will be happy to discuss with you possible alternatives to foreclosure.

Sincerely,

Notice of Intention to Foreclose Sample

NOTICE OF INTENTION TO FORECLOSE
(Under Security Agreement)

To _____ , Debtor

Address_____

You are hereby notified that the undersigned intends to foreclose under provision of that certain Agreement executed by you on the _____ of _____ 20___ , whereby certain personal property described as follows was given as security for the payment of indebtedness to Secured Party named below.

(Description)

You are hereby further notified that unless you pay, within ___ days from the date hereof, to the undersigned, holder and owner of the said Agreement, at their office address, which is listed below, the sum of $_____ , all of which is now due and payable pursuant to the conditions of said Agreement, plus charges at the rate provided for in said Agreement, from date hereof to date of payment, SECURED PARTY SHALL TAKE POSSESSION OF SAID PROPERTY. Further, if said property sells for less than the amount then due under terms of the Agreement, you will be obligated to pay the deficiency.

The Department of Housing and Urban Development offers counseling for homeowners whose mortgage loans have become delinquent. This counseling could help you avoid foreclosure, and you are urged to seek it. To find a homeownership counseling agency near you, please call 1-800-569-4287.

Dated_____ _____
SECURED PARTY

Address_____

_____
By_____

Borrower's Financial Statement (from Fannie Mae - used to evaluate potential Workouts)

FannieMae
BORROWER'S FINANCIAL STATEMENT

	Servicer Loan Number

Property Address	

Is your home listed for sale? Yes ☐ No ☐   Agent's Name: Agent's Phone Number:

Borrower Name	Social Security Number
Mailing Address (#, Street, Apt)	
Mailing Address (City, State, Zip)	
Total number of persons living at this address:	Number of dependents at this address:
Home Phone:	Work Phone:
Co-Borrower Name	Social Security Number
Mailing Address (#, Street, Apt)	
Mailing Address (City, State, Zip)	
Total number of persons living at this address:	Number of dependents at this address:
Home Phone:	Work Phone:
Have you contacted credit counseling services? Yes ☐ No ☐	Number of cars you own?

Monthly Income (Wages): $ _____ / mo.   Additional income (not wages): $ _____ /mo.* Source: _____
*Notice: Alimony, child support or separate maintenance income need not be revealed if the Borrower or Co-Borrower does not choose to have it considered for approval of a loan workout.

Asset Type	Estimated Value	Liability Type	Payment/Month	Balance Due
Home		Alimony/Child Support		
Other Real Estate		Dependent Care		
Checking Accounts		Rent		
Savings/Money Market		Other Mortgage(s)		
IRA/Keogh Accounts		Personal Loan(s)		
401k/ESOP Accounts		Medical Expenses		
Stocks, Bonds, CD's		HOA Fees/Dues		
Other Investments		Other		
Reason for delinquency:				

I (we) agree that the financial information provided is an accurate statement of my (our) financial status. I (we) understand and acknowledge that any action taken by the lender of my (our) mortgage loan on my (our) behalf will be made in strict reliance on the financial information provided. My (Our) signature(s) below grants the holder of my (our) mortgage the authority to confirm the information I (we have disclosed in this financial statement, to verify that it is accurate by ordering a credit report, and to contact my real estate agent and/or credit counseling service representative (if applicable).

Submitted this _____ day of _____, ____.

By: _____   Date: _____
    Signature of Borrower

By: _____   Date: _____
    Signature of Co-Borrower

Before mailing, make sure you have signed and dated the form and attached a copy of your most recent paystub and bank statements of your checking and/or savings account to it. If you are self-employed, attached a copy of your most recent Federal Tax returns.

Page 1 of 1   Fannie Mae Form 1020 11/98

Sample Workout Solicitation Letter (From Fannie Mae - sent with Borrower Financial Stmt)

The mortgage on your home has been turned over to our Loss Mitigation Department. Very little time is left before we must begin the foreclosure process.

Help us save your home...
- You may be eligible for an alternative to foreclosure.
- We may be able to assist you if you have financial hardship.

Possible Hardships:
- Are you unemployed, or are you experiencing a substantial cut in pay?
- Is a family member deceased or seriously ill?
- Has a divorce affected your ability to make the mortgage payments?
- Have you had to relocate due to loss of employment?

If you answered "YES" to any of these questions, we may be able to help you.

If you can afford to keep your home...
- We may be able to adjust your monthly payment for a specific time to help you bring the loan current; or
- We may be able to modify the terms of your loan to make it more affordable.

If you *cannot* afford to keep your home...
- We may allow a qualified buyer to assume your loan.
- If you sell your home at market value and the value is less than the total due, we may agree to accept the sale proceeds to satisfy some or all of the amount owed.
- We may allow you to voluntarily deed the property back to us to satisfy some or all of the amount you owe. This would enable you to avoid a public foreclosure sale.

If you are like most people, homeownership is important to you. If you want help finding a solution to cure your defaulted loan, take the following actions today!
- Complete the enclosed one-page Borrower's Financial Statement.
- Attach supporting documentation listed at the end of the financial statement.
- Mail the completed package to the attention of [Your Name] at the address provided.

We look forward to working with you and will be contacting you soon!
If you have any questions, please contact me at 1.800.555.1212.

Important Note: Contacting our office will not suspend your obligation to make your mortgage payments. Furthermore, we will continue all collection efforts and foreclosure activity unless and until a workout plan has been completed.

Notice Required by Fair Debt Collection Practices Act

NOTICE REQUIRED BY THE
FAIR DEBT COLLECTION PRACTICES ACT,
15 U.S.C. SECTION 1692 AS AMENDED

1.   The amount of the debts is the amount described in the complaint.

2.   The Plaintiff is the creditor to whom the debt is owed.

3.   The debt will be assumed to be valid by the creditor's law firm, unless the consumer(s) within thirty (30) days after the receipt of this notice, disputes, in writing, the validity of the debt or some portion thereof.

4.   If the consumer(s) notifies the creditor's law firm in writing within (30) days of the receipt of this notice that the debt or any portion thereof is disputed, the creditor's law firm will obtain verification of the debt and copy of the judgment against the consumer(s) and mail such verification or a copy of the judgment to the consumer(s)

5.   If the creditor named as Plaintiff in the complaint is not the original creditor, and if the consumer(s) makes a written request to the creditor's law firm within thirty (30) days from the receipt of this notice, the name and address of the original creditor will be mailed to the consumer(s) by the creditor's law firm.

6.   Written requests should be addressed to _____.

7.   This is an attempt to collect a debt, and any information obtained will be used for that purpose.

IRS Form 1099-A Acquisition or Abandonment of Secured Property

☐ CORRECTED (if checked)

LENDER'S name, street address, city or town, province or state, country, ZIP or foreign postal code, and telephone no.		OMB No. 1545-0877 20**13** Form **1099-A**	**Acquisition or Abandonment of Secured Property**
	1 Date of lender's acquisition or knowledge of abandonment	**2** Balance of principal outstanding $	**Copy B For Borrower**
LENDER'S federal identification number	BORROWER'S identification number		
	3	**4** Fair market value of property $	This is important tax information and is being furnished to the Internal Revenue Service. If you are required to file a
BORROWER'S name			return, a negligence
Street address (including apt. no.)	**5** If checked, the borrower was personally liable for repayment of the debt . . . . ▶ ☐		sanction may be imposed on you if
City or town, province or state, country, and ZIP or foreign postal code	**6** Description of property		taxable income results from this transaction and the IRS determines
Account number (see instructions)			that it has not been reported.

Form **1099-A**   (keep for your records)   www.irs.gov/form1099a   Department of the Treasury - Internal Revenue Service

IRS Form 1099-C Cancellation of Debt

☐ CORRECTED (if checked)

CREDITOR'S name, street address, city or town, province or state, country, ZIP, or foreign postal code, and telephone no.		**1** Date of identifiable event	OMB No. 1545-1424	**Cancellation of Debt**
		2 Amount of debt discharged $	20**13**	
		3 Interest if included in box 2 $	Form **1099-C**	
CREDITOR'S federal identification number	DEBTOR'S identification number	**4** Debt description		**Copy B**
DEBTOR'S name				**For Debtor** This is important tax information and is being furnished to the Internal Revenue Service. If you are required to file a
Street address (including apt. no.)		**5** If checked, the debtor was personally liable for repayment of the debt . . . . ▶ ☐		return, a negligence penalty or other sanction may be imposed on you if
City or town, province or state, country, and ZIP or foreign postal code				taxable income results from this transaction and the IRS determines
Account number (see instructions)		**6** Identifiable event code	**7** Fair market value of property $	that it has not been reported.

Form **1099-C**   (keep for your records)   www.irs.gov/form1099c   Department of the Treasury - Internal Revenue Service

Notice to Users of Consumer Reports - FTC Disclosure

NOTICE TO USERS OF CONSUMER REPORTS
Obligations of Users Under the FCRA

The federal Fair Credit Reporting Act (FCRA) requires that this notice be provided to inform users of consumer reports of their legal obligations. State law may impose additional requirements. This first section of this summary sets forth the responsibilities imposed by the FCRA on all users of consumer reports. The subsequent sections discuss the duties of users of reports that contain specific types of information, or that are used for certain purposes, and the legal consequences of violations. The FCRA, 15 U.S.C. 1681-1681u, is set forth in full at the Federal Trade Commission's Internet web site (http://www.ftc.gov).

I. OBLIGATIONS OF ALL USERS OF CONSUMER REPORTS
A. Users Must Have a Permissible Purpose
Congress has limited the use of consumer reports to protect consumers' privacy. All users must have a permissible purpose under the FCRA to obtain a consumer report. Section 604 of the FCRA contains a list of the permissible purposes under the law. These are:

☐ As ordered by a court or a federal grand jury subpoena. *Section 604(a)(1)*

☐ As instructed by the consumer in writing. *Section 604(a)(2)*

☐ For the extension of credit as a result of an application from a consumer, or the review or collection of a consumer's account. *Section 604(a)(3)(A)*

☐ For employment purposes, including hiring and promotion decisions, where the consumer has given written permission. *Sections 604(a)(3)(B) and 604(b)*

☐ For the underwriting of insurance as a result of an application from a consumer. *Section 604(a)(3)(C)*

☐ When there is a legitimate business need, in connection with a business transaction that is initiated by the consumer. *Section 604(a)(3)(F)(i)*

☐ To review a consumer's account to determine whether the consumer continues to meet the terms of the account. *Section 604(a)(3)(F)(ii)*

☐ To determine a consumer's eligibility for a license or other benefit granted by a governmental instrumentality required by law to consider an applicant's financial responsibility or status. *Section 604(a)(3)(D)*

☐ For use by a potential investor or servicer, or current insurer, in a valuation or assessment of the credit or prepayment risks associated with an existing credit obligation. *Section 604(a)(3)(E)*

☐ For use by state and local officials in connection with the determination of child support payments, or modifications and enforcement thereof. *Sections 604(a)(4) and 604(a)(5)*

In addition, creditors and insurers may obtain certain consumer report information for the purpose of making unsolicited offers of credit or insurance. The particular obligations of users of this "prescreened" information are described in Section V below.

B. Users Must Provide Certifications
Section 604(f) of the FCRA prohibits any person from obtaining a consumer report from a consumer reporting agency (CRA) unless the person has certified to the CRA (by a general or specific certification, as appropriate) the permissible purpose(s) for which the report is being obtained and certifies that the report will not be used for any other purpose.

C. Users Must Notify Consumers When Adverse Actions Are Taken

The term "adverse action" is defined very broadly by Section 603 of the FCRA. "Adverse actions" include all business, credit, and employment actions affecting consumers that can be considered to have a negative impact -- such as unfavorably changing credit or contract terms or conditions, denying or canceling credit or insurance, offering credit on less favorable terms than requested, or denying employment or promotion.

1. Adverse Actions Based on Information Obtained From a CRA

If a user takes any type of adverse action that is based at least in part on information contained in a consumer report, the user is required by Section 615(a) of the FCRA to notify the consumer. The notification may be done in writing, orally, or by electronic means. It must include the following:

1. The name, address, and telephone number of the CRA (including a toll-free telephone number, if it is a nationwide CRA) that provided the report.

2. A statement that the CRA did not make the adverse decision and is not able to explain why the decision was made.

3. A statement setting forth the consumer's right to obtain a free disclosure of the consumer's file from the CRA if the consumer requests the report within 60 days.

4. A statement setting forth the consumer's right to dispute directly with the CRA the accuracy or completeness of any information provided by the CRA.

2. Adverse Actions Based on Information Obtained From Third Parties Who Are Not Consumer Reporting Agencies

If a person denies (or increases the charge for) credit for personal, family, or household purposes based either wholly or partly upon information from a person other than a CRA, and the information is the type of consumer information covered by the FCRA, Section 615(b)(1) of the FCRA requires that the user clearly and accurately disclose to the consumer his or her right to obtain disclosure of the nature of the information that was relied upon by making a written request within 60 days of notification. The user must provide the disclosure within a reasonable period of time following the consumer's written request.

3. Adverse Actions Based on Information Obtained From Affiliates

If a person takes an adverse action involving insurance, employment, or a credit transaction initiated by the consumer, based on information of the type covered by the FCRA, and this information was obtained from an entity affiliated with the user of the information by common ownership or control, Section 615(b)(2) requires the user to notify the consumer of the adverse action. The notification must inform the consumer that he or she may obtain a disclosure of the nature of the information relied upon by making a written request within 60 days of receiving the adverse action notice. If the consumer makes such a request, the user must disclose the nature of the information not later than 30 days after receiving the request. (Information that is obtained directly from an affiliated entity relating solely to its transactions or experiences with the consumer, and information from a consumer report obtained from an affiliate are not covered by Section 615(b)(2).)

II. OBLIGATIONS OF USERS WHEN CONSUMER REPORTS ARE OBTAINED FOR EMPLOYMENT PURPOSES

If information from a CRA is used for employment purposes, the user has specific duties, which are set forth in Section 604(b) of the FCRA. The user must:

1. Make a clear and conspicuous written disclosure to the consumer before the report is obtained, in a document that consists solely of the disclosure, that a consumer report may be obtained.

2. Obtain prior written authorization from the consumer.

3. Certify to the CRA that the above steps have been followed, that the information being obtained will not be used in violation of any federal or state equal opportunity law or regulation, and that, if any adverse action is to be taken based on the consumer report, a copy of the report and a summary of the consumer's rights will be provided to the consumer.

4. Before taking an adverse action, provide a copy of the report to the consumer as well as the summary of the consumer's rights.

(The user should receive this summary from the CRA, because Section 604(b)(1)(B) of the FCRA requires CRAs to provide a copy of the summary with each consumer report obtained for employment purposes.)

III. OBLIGATIONS OF USERS OF INVESTIGATIVE CONSUMER REPORTS

Investigative consumer reports are a special type of consumer report in which information about a consumer's character, general reputation, personal characteristics, and mode of living is obtained through personal interviews. Consumers who are the subjects of such reports are given special rights under the FCRA. If a user intends to obtain an investigative consumer report, Section 606 of the FCRA requires the following:

1. The user must disclose to the consumer that an investigative consumer report may be obtained. This must be done in a written disclosure that is mailed, or otherwise delivered, to the consumer not later than three days after the date on which the report was first requested. The disclosure must include a statement informing the consumer of his or her right to request additional disclosures of the nature and scope of the investigation as described below, and must include the summary of consumer rights required by Section 609 of the FCRA. (The user should be able to obtain a copy of the notice of consumer rights from the CRA that provided the consumer report.)

2. The user must certify to the CRA that the disclosures set forth above have been made and that the user will make the disclosure described below.

3. Upon the written request of a consumer made within a reasonable period of time after the disclosures required above, the user must make a complete disclosure of the nature and scope of the investigation that was requested. This must be made in a written statement that is mailed, or otherwise delivered, to the consumer no later than five days after the date on which the request was received from the consumer or the report was first requested, whichever is later in time.

OBLIGATIONS OF USERS OF CONSUMER REPORTS CONTAINING MEDICAL INFORMATION

Section 604(g) of the FCRA prohibits consumer reporting agencies from providing consumer reports that contain medical information for employment purposes, or in connection with credit or insurance transactions, without the specific prior consent of the consumer who is the subject of the report. In the case of medical information being sought for employment purposes, the consumer must explicitly consent to the release of the medical information in addition to authorizing the obtaining of a consumer report generally.

V. OBLIGATIONS OF USERS OF "PRESCREENED" LISTS

The FCRA permits creditors and insurers to obtain limited consumer report information for use in connection with unsolicited offers of credit or insurance under certain circumstances. *Sections 603(l), 604(c), 604(e), and 615(d)* This practice is known as "prescreening" and typically involves obtaining a list of consumers from a CRA who meet certain preestablished criteria. If any person intends to use prescreened lists, that person must (1) before the offer is made, establish the criteria that will be relied upon to make the offer and to grant credit or insurance, and (2) maintain such criteria on file for a three-year period beginning on the date on which the offer is made to each consumer. In addition, any user must provide with each written solicitation a clear and conspicuous statement that:

1. Information contained in a consumer's CRA file was used in connection with the transaction.

2. The consumer received the offer because he or she satisfied the criteria for credit worthiness or insurability used to screen for the offer.

3. Credit or insurance may not be extended if, after the consumer responds, it is determined that the consumer does not meet the criteria used for screening or any applicable criteria bearing on credit worthiness or insurability, or the consumer does not furnish required collateral.

4. The consumer may prohibit the use of information in his or her file in connection with future prescreened offers of credit or insurance by contacting the notification system established by the CRA that provided the report. This statement must include the address and toll-free telephone number of the appropriate notification system.

VI. OBLIGATIONS OF RESELLERS

Section 607(e) of the FCRA requires any person who obtains a consumer report for resale to take the following steps:

1. Disclose the identity of the end-user to the source CRA.

2. Identify to the source CRA each permissible purpose for which the report will be furnished to the end-user.

3. Establish and follow reasonable procedures to ensure that reports are resold only for permissible purposes, including procedures to obtain:

> (1) the identity of all end-users;
> (2) certifications from all users of each purpose for which reports will be used; and
> (3) certifications that reports will not be used for any purpose other than the purpose(s) specified to the reseller. Resellers must make reasonable efforts to verify this information before selling the report.

VII. LIABILITY FOR VIOLATIONS OF THE FCRA

Failure to comply with the FCRA can result in state or federal enforcement actions, as well as private lawsuits. *Sections 616, 617, and 621.* In addition, any person who knowingly and willfully obtains a consumer report under false pretenses may face criminal prosecution. *Section 619*

Sample Truth in Lending Disclosure Statement

TRUTH IN LENDING DISCLOSURE STATEMENT

Creditor	Applicant(s)
Mailing Address	Property Address
Loan Number	Preparation Date

ANNUAL PERCENTAGE RATE The cost of your credit as a yearly rate.	FINANCE CHARGE The dollar amount the credit will cost you.	Amount Financed The amount of credit provided to you or on your behalf.	Total of Payments The amount you will have paid after you have made all payments as scheduled.
E %	ES	ES	ES

PAYMENT SCHEDULE:

NUMBER OF PAYMENTS	* AMOUNT OF PAYMENTS	MONTHLY PAYMENTS ARE DUE BEGINNING	NUMBER OF PAYMENTS	* AMOUNT OF PAYMENTS	MONTHLY PAYMENTS ARE DUE BEGINNING

* Includes mortgage insurance premiums, excludes taxes, hazard insurance or flood insurance.

DEMAND FEATURE: ☐ This loan does not have a Demand Feature   ☐ This loan has a Demand Feature.

ITEMIZATION: You have a right at this time to an ITEMIZATION OF AMOUNT FINANCED.
I/We ☐ do ☐ do not want an itemization.

REQUIRED DEPOSIT:
☐ The annual percentage rate does not take into account your required deposit.

VARIABLE RATE FEATURE:
☐ This Loan has a Variable Rate Feature. Variable Rate Disclosures have been provided to you earlier.

SECURITY: You are giving a security interest in:

ASSUMPTION: Someone buying this property
☐ cannot assume the remaining balance due under original mortgage terms.
☐ may assume, subject to lender's conditions, the remaining balance due under original mortgage terms.

FILING / RECORDING FEES: S

PROPERTY INSURANCE:
☐ Property / hazard insurance is a required condition of this loan. Borrower may purchase this insurance from any insurance company acceptable to the lender.
Hazard Insurance ☐ is ☐ is not available through the lender at an estimated cost of   for a   month term.

LATE CHARGES: If your payment is more than   days late, you will be charged a late charge of   % of the overdue payment.

PREPAYMENT: If you prepay this loan in full or in part, you
☐ may ☐ will not have to pay a penalty.
☐ may ☐ will not be entitled to a refund of part of the finance charge.

See your contract documents for any additional information regarding non-payment, default, required repayment in full before scheduled date, and payment refunds and penalties.
E means estimate.

I/We hereby acknowledge reading and receiving a complete copy of this disclosure. I/We understand there is no commitment for the creditor to make this loan and there is no obligation for me/us to accept this loan upon delivery or signing of this disclosure.

_____   Date   _____   Date

_____   Date   _____   Date

HUD-1 Settlement Statement (available at www.hud.gov)

A. **Settlement Statement**	U.S. Department of Housing and Urban Development	OMB Approval No. 2502-0265

B. Type of Loan

1. ☐ FHA 2. ☐ FmHA 3. ☐ Conv. Unins. 4. ☐ VA 5. ☐ Conv. Ins.	6. File Number:	7. Loan Number:	8. Mortgage Insurance Case Number:

C. Note: This form is furnished to give you a statement of actual settlement costs. Amounts paid to and by the settlement agent are shown. Items marked "(p.o.c.)" were paid outside the closing; they are shown here for informational purposes and are not included in the totals.

D. Name & Address of Borrower:	E. Name & Address of Seller:	F. Name & Address of Lender:

| G. Property Location: | H. Settlement Agent: | |
| | Place of Settlement: | I. Settlement Date: |

J. Summary of Borrower's Transaction		K. Summary of Seller's Transaction	
100. Gross Amount Due From Borrower		**400. Gross Amount Due To Seller**	
101. Contract sales price		401. Contract sales price	
102. Personal property		402. Personal property	
103. Settlement charges to borrower (line 1400)		403.	
104.		404.	
105.		405.	
Adjustments for items paid by seller in advance		**Adjustments for items paid by seller in advance**	
106. City/town taxes to		406. City/town taxes to	
107. County taxes to		407. County taxes to	
108. Assessments to		408. Assessments to	
109.		409.	
110.		410.	
111.		411.	
112.		412.	
120. Gross Amount Due From Borrower		**420. Gross Amount Due To Seller**	
200. Amounts Paid By Or In Behalf Of Borrower		**500. Reductions In Amount Due To Seller**	
201. Deposit or earnest money		501. Excess deposit (see instructions)	
202. Principal amount of new loan(s)		502. Settlement charges to seller (line 1400)	
203. Existing loan(s) taken subject to		503. Existing loan(s) taken subject to	
204.		504. Payoff of first mortgage loan	
205.		505. Payoff of second mortgage loan	
206.		506.	
207.		507.	
208.		508.	
209.		509.	
Adjustments for items unpaid by seller		**Adjustments for items unpaid by seller**	
210. City/town taxes to		510. City/town taxes to	
211. County taxes to		511. County taxes to	
212. Assessments to		512. Assessments to	
213.		513.	
214.		514.	
215.		515.	
216.		516.	
217.		517.	
218.		518.	
219.		519.	
220. Total Paid By/For Borrower		**520. Total Reduction Amount Due Seller**	
300. Cash At Settlement From/To Borrower		**600. Cash At Settlement To/From Seller**	
301. Gross Amount due from borrower (line 120)		601. Gross amount due to seller (line 420)	
302. Less amounts paid by/for borrower (line 220)	( )	602. Less reductions in amt. due seller (line 520)	( )
303. Cash ☐ From ☐ To Borrower		**603. Cash ☐ To ☐ From Seller**	

Section 5 of the Real Estate Settlement Procedures Act (RESPA) requires the following: • HUD must develop a Special Information Booklet to help persons borrowing money to finance the purchase of residential real estate to better understand the nature and costs of real estate settlement services; • Each lender must provide the booklet to all applicants from whom it receives or for whom it prepares a written application to borrow money to finance the purchase of residential real estate; • Lenders must prepare and distribute with the Booklet a Good Faith Estimate of the settlement costs that the borrower is likely to incur in connection with the settlement. These disclosures are manadatory.

Section 4(a) of RESPA mandates that HUD develop and prescribe this standard form to be used at the time of loan settlement to provide full disclosure of all charges imposed upon the borrower and seller. These are third party disclosures that are designed to provide the borrower with pertinent information during the settlement process in order to be a better shopper.

The Public Reporting Burden for this collection of information is estimated to average one hour per response, including the time for reviewing instructions, searching existing data sources, gathering and maintaining the data needed, and completing and reviewing the collection of information.

This agency may not collect this information, and you are not required to complete this form, unless it displays a currently valid OMB control number.

The information requested does not lend itself to confidentiality.

L. Settlement Charges

700. Total Sales/Broker's Commission based on price $ @ % =		Paid From Borrowers Funds at Settlement	Paid From Seller's Funds at Settlement
Division of Commission (line 700) as follows:			
701. $	to		
702. $	to		
703. Commission paid at Settlement			
704.			
800. Items Payable In Connection With Loan			
801. Loan Origination Fee	%		
802. Loan Discount	%		
803. Appraisal Fee	to		
804. Credit Report	to		
805. Lender's Inspection Fee			
806. Mortgage Insurance Application Fee to			
807. Assumption Fee			
808.			
809.			
810.			
811.			
900. Items Required By Lender To Be Paid In Advance			
901. Interest from to @$ /day			
902. Mortgage Insurance Premium for months to			
903. Hazard Insurance Premium for years to			
904. years to			
905.			
1000. Reserves Deposited With Lender			
1001. Hazard insurance	months@$ per month		
1002. Mortgage insurance	months@$ per month		
1003. City property taxes	months@$ per month		
1004. County property taxes	months@$ per month		
1005. Annual assessments	months@$ per month		
1006.	months@$ per month		
1007.	months@$ per month		
1008.	months@$ per month		
1100. Title Charges			
1101. Settlement or closing fee	to		
1102. Abstract or title search	to		
1103. Title examination	to		
1104. Title insurance binder	to		
1105. Document preparation	to		
1106. Notary fees	to		
1107. Attorney's fees	to		
(includes above items numbers:)			
1108. Title insurance	to		
(includes above items numbers:)			
1109. Lender's coverage	$		
1110. Owner's coverage	$		
1111.			
1112.			
1113.			
1200. Government Recording and Transfer Charges			
1201. Recording fees: Deed $; Mortgage $; Releases $			
1202. City/county tax/stamps: Deed $; Mortgage $			
1203. State tax/stamps: Deed $; Mortgage $			
1204.			
1205.			
1300. Additional Settlement Charges			
1301. Survey to			
1302. Pest Inspection to			
1303.			
1304.			
1305.			
1400. Total Settlement Charges (enter on lines 103, Section J and 502, Section K)			

Seller Disclosure of Condition (Sample Texas Form)

APPROVED BY THE TEXAS REAL ESTATE COMMISSION (TREC)   10-25-93

SELLER'S DISCLOSURE OF PROPERTY CONDITION

(SECTION 5.008, TEXAS PROPERTY CODE)

CONCERNING THE PROPERTY AT_____
(Street Address and City)

THIS NOTICE IS A DISCLOSURE OF SELLER'S KNOWLEDGE OF THE CONDITION OF THE PROPERTY AS OF THE DATE SIGNED BY SELLER AND IS NOT A SUBSTITUTE FOR ANY INSPECTIONS OR WARRANTIES THE PURCHASER MAY WISH TO OBTAIN. IT IS NOT A WARRANTY OF ANY KIND BY SELLER OR SELLER'S AGENTS.

Seller ☐ is ☐ is not occupying the Property. If unoccupied, how long since Seller has occupied the Property? _____

1. The Property has the items checked below [Write Yes (Y), No (N), or Unknown (U)]:

Range	Oven	Microwave
Dishwasher	Trash Compactor	Disposal
Washer/Dryer Hookups	Window Screens	Rain Gutters
Security System	Fire Detection Equipment	Intercom System
TV Antenna	Cable TV Wiring	Satellite Dish
Ceiling Fan(s)	Attic Fan(s)	Exhaust Fan(s)
Central A/C	Central Heating	Wall/Window Air Conditioning
Plumbing System	Septic System	Public Sewer System
Patio/Decking	Outdoor Grill	Fences
Pool	Sauna	Spa___Hot Tub
Pool Equipment	Pool Heater	Automatic Lawn Sprinkler System
Fireplace(s) & Chimney(Woodburning)	Fireplace(s) & Chimney (Mock)	Gas Lines (Nat./LP)
Gas Fixtures	Garage:___Attached ___Not Attached	Carport
Garage Door Opener(s):	Electronic	Control(s)
Water Heater:	Gas	Electric
Water Supply:___City	Well	MUD ___Co-op

Roof Type:_____ Age:_____(approx)

Are you (Seller) aware of any of the above items that are not in working condition, that have known defects, or that are in need of repair? ☐ Yes ☐ No ☐ Unknown. If yes, then describe. (Attach additional sheets if necessary): _____

2. Are you (Seller) aware of any known defects/malfunctions in any of the following? Write Yes (Y) if you are aware, write No (N) if you are not aware.

Interior Walls	Ceilings	Floors
Exterior Walls	Doors	Windows
Roof	Foundation/Slab(s)	Basement
Walls/Fences	Driveways	Sidewalks
Plumbing/Sewers/Septics	Electrical Systems	Lighting Fixtures
Other Structural Components (Describe)		

Seller's Disclosure Notice Concerning the Property at_____ Page 2   10-25-93
                                      (Street Address and City)

If the answer to any of the above is yes, explain. (Attach additional sheets if necessary): _____

_____

3. Are you (Seller) aware of any of the following conditions? Write Yes (Y) if you are aware, write No (N) if you are not aware.

___Active Termites (includes wood-   ___Termite or Wood Rot Damage   ___Previous Termite Damage
       destroying insects)   Needing Repair

___Previous Termite Treatment   ___Previous Flooding   ___Improper Drainage

___Water Penetration   ___Located in 100-Year Floodplain   ___Present Flood Insurance
                                                                                         Coverage

___Previous Structural or Roof   ___Hazardous or Toxic Waste   ___Asbestos Components
       Repair

___Urea-formaldehyde Insulation   ___Radon Gas   ___Lead Based Paint
___Aluminum Wiring   ___Previous Fires   ___Unplatted Easements
___Landfill, Settling, Soil   ___Subsurface Structure or Pits
       Movement, Fault Lines

If the answer to any of the above is yes, explain. (Attach additional sheets if necessary): _____

_____

4. Are you (Seller) aware of any item, equipment, or system in or on the Property that is in need of repair? ☐ Yes (if
    you are aware) ☐ No (if you are not aware). If yes, explain (attach additional sheets as necessary). _____

_____

5. Are you (Seller) aware of any of the following? Write Yes (Y) if you are aware, write No (N) if you are not aware.

    ___   Room additions, structural modifications, or other alterations or repairs made without necessary permits or not in compliance
           with building codes in effect at that time.

    ___   Homeowners' Association or maintenance fees or assessments.

    ___   Any "common area" (facilities such as pools, tennis courts, walkways, or other areas) co-owned in undivided interest with
           others.

    ___   Any notices of violations of deed restrictions or governmental ordinances affecting the condition or use of the Property.

    ___   Any lawsuits directly or indirectly affecting the Property.

    ___   Any condition on the Property which materially affects the physical health or safety of an individual.

If the answer to any of the above is yes, explain. (Attach additional sheets if necessary): _____

_____

Date _____ Signature of Seller _____ Date _____ Signature of Seller _____

The undersigned purchaser hereby acknowledges receipt of the foregoing notice.

Date _____ Signature of Purchaser _____ Date _____ Signature of Purchaser _____

IRS Form 1098 Mortgage Interest Statement

8181 □ VOID □ CORRECTED

RECIPIENT'S/LENDER'S name, address, and telephone number		OMB No. 1545-0901	**Mortgage Interest Statement**
		2013 Form **1098**	

RECIPIENT'S federal identification no.	PAYER'S social security number	**1** Mortgage interest received from payer(s)/borrower(s) $	**Copy A**
PAYER'S/BORROWER'S name		**2** Points paid on purchase of principal residence $	**For Internal Revenue Service Center** File with Form 1096. For Privacy Act
Street address (including apt. no.)		**3** Refund of overpaid interest $	and Paperwork Reduction Act Notice, see the
City, state, and ZIP code		**4** Mortgage insurance premiums $	**2009 General Instructions for**
Account number (see instructions)		**5**	**Forms 1099, 1098, 3921, 3922, 5498, and W-2G.**

Form **1098** Cat. No. 14402K Department of the Treasury - Internal Revenue Service

Do Not Cut or Separate Forms on This Page — Do Not Cut or Separate Forms on This Page

IRS Form 1096 Annual Summary and Transmittal of Returns

Do Not Staple   6969

Form **1096** Department of the Treasury Internal Revenue Service	**Annual Summary and Transmittal of U.S. Information Returns**	OMB No. 1545-0108 2013

FILER'S name

Street address (including room or suite number)

City, state, and ZIP code

Name of person to contact	Telephone number ( )	**For Official Use Only**
Email address	Fax number ( )	□□□□□□□ □□

1 Employer identification number	2 Social security number	3 Total number of forms	4 Federal income tax withheld $	5 Total amount reported with this Form 1096 $

6 Enter an "X" in only one box below to indicate the type of form being filed.

7 If this is your **final return**, enter an "X" here . . . ▶ □

W-2G 32	1098 81	1098-C 78	1098-E 84	1098-T 83	1099-A 80	1099-B 79	1099-C 85	1099-CAP 73	1099-DIV 91	1099-G 86	1099-H 71	1099-INT 92	1099-LTC 93
□	□	□	□	□	□	□	□	□	□	□	□	□	□

1099-MISC 95	1099-OID 96	1099-PATR 97	1099-Q 31	1099-R 98	1099-S 75	1099-SA 94	3921 25	3922 26	5498 28	5498-ESA 72	5498-SA 27		
□	□	□	□	□	□	□	□	□	□	□	□		

Return this entire page to the Internal Revenue Service. Photocopies are not acceptable.

Under penalties of perjury, I declare that I have examined this return and accompanying documents, and, to the best of my knowledge and belief, they are true, correct, and complete.

Signature ▶   Title ▶   Date ▶

Appendix C
DELINQUENT
SERVICING SCHEDULE

(Source: Fannie Mae)

Number of Days Delinquent	Low Risk Mortgage	High Risk Mortgage
Day 16	Send late payment notice	Send late payment notice
Day 17-20		Make initial telephone contact*
Day 35		Send breech letter unless progress is being made to resolve delinquency**
Day 40	Make initial telephone contact*	
Day 50	Send workout solicitation letter and Borrower's Financial Statement	Send workout solicitation letter and Borrower's Financial Statement
Day 62	Send breech letter unless progress is being made to resolve delinquency**	
Day 80-95		Initiate foreclosure 30-45 days after breech letter.
Day 91-107	Initiate foreclosure 30-45 days after breech letter.	

* Earlier for borrowers who are habitually delinquent.
** Earlier for abandoned properties or borrowers who exhibit lack of concern for mortgage obligation.
■Days refer to the number of days past the due date of the first missed payment.

INDEX